THE BASEBALL GLOVE

The baseball glove is a ubiquitous item, a crucial piece of equipment in the game of baseball, and it offers the opportunity to examine the production of material culture and social practice at numerous levels. Where and how is a glove made, and how does its manufacture square with the narratives surrounding its place in American cultural life? What are the myths, superstitions, and beliefs surrounding its acquisition, care, use, and significance? How does a glove function as the center of a web of cultural practices that illustrate how individuals relate to a consumer good as a symbol of memory, personal narrative, and national identity? How do the manufacturers of baseball gloves draw upon, promote, and in some sense create these practices? How do these practices and meanings change in other national and cultural contexts?

The Baseball Glove offers students the opportunity to examine these questions in an engagingly written and illustrated book that promotes hands-on interaction with a quintessential item of material culture. At the same time, the book gives students the space for critical self-reflection about the place of material goods like sporting equipment in their lives, and it provides the chance to learn different methodological approaches to studying everyday objects.

David Jenemann is Associate Professor in the Department of English's program in film and television studies at the University of Vermont.

The Routledge Series for Creative Teaching and Learning in Anthropology
Editor: Richard H. Robbins, SUNY Plattsburgh and
Luis A. Vivanco, University of Vermont

This series is dedicated to innovative, unconventional ways to connect undergraduate students and their lived concerns about our social world to the power of social science ideas and evidence. We seek to publish titles that use anthropology to help students understand how they benefit from exposing their own lives and activities to the power of anthropological thought and analysis. Our goal is to help spark social science imaginations and, in doing so, open new avenues for meaningful thought and action.

   Books in this series pose questions and problems that speak to the complexities and dynamism of modern life, connecting cutting edge research in exciting and relevant topical areas with creative pedagogy.

Available

The Baseball Glove
History, Material, Meaning, and Value
David Jenemann

Persian Carpets
The Nation as a Transnational Commodity
Minoo Moallem

An Anthropology of Money
A Critical Introduction
Tim Di Muzio and Richard H. Robbins

Coffee Culture, 2e
Local Experiences, Global Connections
Catherine M. Tucker

Re-Imagining Milk, 2e
Cultural and Biological Perspectives
Andrea S. Wiley

Forthcoming

Seafood
From Ocean to Plate
Richard Wilk & Shingo Hamada

Love Letters
Saving Romance in the Digital Age
Michelle Janning

THE BASEBALL GLOVE

History, Material, Meaning, and Value

David Jenemann

Routledge
Taylor & Francis Group

NEW YORK AND LONDON

First published 2018
by Routledge
711 Third Avenue, New York, NY 10017

and by Routledge
2 Park Square, Milton Park, Abingdon, Oxon, OX14 4RN

Routledge is an imprint of the Taylor & Francis Group, an informa business

Library of Congress Cataloging-in-Publication Data
Names: Jenemann, David, 1971- author.
Title: The baseball glove: history, material, meaning,
and value/David Jenemann.
Description: New York, NY: Routledge, 2018. | Series: The Routledge
series for creative teaching and learning in anthropology |
Includes bibliographical references and index.
Identifiers: LCCN 2017059116 (print) | LCCN 2018005570 (ebook) |
ISBN 9781315526737 (Master Ebook) | ISBN 9781315526720 (Web pdf) |
ISBN 9781315526713 (ePub) | ISBN 9781315526706 (Mobipocket) |
ISBN 9781138682030 (hardback: alk. paper) | ISBN 9781138682047
(pbk.: alk. paper)
Subjects: LCSH: Baseball gloves.
Classification: LCC GV879.7 (ebook) | LCC GV879.7.J46 2018 (print) |
DDC 796.357028/4–dc23
LC record available at https://lccn.loc.gov/2017059116

ISBN: 978-1-138-68203-0 (hbk)
ISBN: 978-1-138-68204-7 (pbk)
ISBN: 978-1-315-52673-7 (ebk)

Typeset in New Baskerville
by Sunrise Setting Ltd, Brixham, UK

For Don Wright

CONTENTS

SERIES FOREWORD

The premise of these short books on the anthropology of stuff is that stuff talks, that written into the biographies of everyday items of our lives—coffee, T-shirts, computers, iPods, flowers, drugs, and so forth—are the stories that make us who we are and that make the world the way it is. From their beginnings, each item bears the signature of the people who extracted, manufactured, picked, caught, assembled, packaged, delivered, purchased, and disposed of it. And in our modern market-driven societies, our lives are dominated by the pursuit of stuff.

Examining stuff is also an excellent way to teach and learn about what is exciting and insightful about anthropological and sociological ways of knowing. Students, as with virtually all of us, can relate to stuff, while at the same time discovering through these books that it can provide new and fascinating ways of looking at the world. ·

Stuff, or commodities and things, are central, of course, to all societies, to one extent or another. Whether it is yams, necklaces, horses, cattle, or shells, the acquisition, accumulation, and exchange of things is central to the identities and relationships that tie people together and drive their behavior. But never, before now, has the craving for stuff reached the level it has; and never before have so many people been trying to convince each other that acquiring more stuff is what they most want to do. As a consequence, the creation, consumption, and disposal of stuff now threaten the planet itself. Yet to stop or even slow down the manufacture and accumulation of stuff would threaten the viability of our economy, on which our society is built.

This raises various questions. For example, what impact does the compulsion to acquire stuff have on our economic, social, and political well-being, as well as on our environment? How do we come to believe that there are certain things that we must have? How do we come to value some commodities or form of commodities above others? How have we managed to create commodity chains that link peasant farmers in Colombia or gold miners in Angola to wealthy residents of New York or teenagers in Nebraska? Who comes up with the ideas for stuff and how do they translate those ideas into things for people to buy? Why do we sometimes consume stuff that is not very good for us? These short books examine such questions, and more.

FOREWORD
by Bill Lee

Necessity is the mother of invention!

Recently, I played in a vintage baseball league with Jim Bouton, of New York Yankees and *Ball Four* fame. When we played a July 4th game in Pittsfield, Massachusetts between my 1881 Hartford Senators and Jim's Pittsfield Hillies, I had a catcher named Grit.

He had the best hands, toughest I have ever seen. I had played with George "Boomer" Scott; I had played with Luis Aparicio, both excellent fielders. They had ball gloves. Grit had a brakeman's glove. It had a small pad protecting his left palm. Before 1881, the glove was whatever you invented to protect against the variety of breaks, sprains, and other injuries you would most likely endure. That's what Grit wore. And that is how it all started.

The baseball glove! I have always said baseball is the belly button of the earth. Through this timeless game of 27 outs and 9 innings, we will find world peace. This book on the glove rivals Joseph Campbell's *The Power of Myth* and Campbell didn't even like baseball! Take a look at Dave's photo of gloves on the field in Havana, Cuba (Figure 0.1). Marshall McLuhan once said that all forms of communication are forms of persuasion. This photograph shows what is right with baseball. It is a pile of gloves worn by Cuban youth players. Some of the gloves were brought by their American counterparts to be left in Cuba after a week of games. Late in the 1800s and early 1900s, gloves were left in the outfield at the end of the half inning. They were flat like mine (see Figure 0.3). The players didn't trip up the opposing team; sometimes they even shared gloves.

Nobody wanted to share William Francis Lee Senior's glove. My grandfather played on a precursor to the Hollywood Stars around 1918. He was one of the best second basemen in the league and had the nickname "No Touch" before the Hall of Fame second baseman Bill Mazeroski did. He would cut the leather out of the palm of his glove to make his hands quicker and softer. This would help him turn the double play. Bobby Doerr, who just passed away in 2017, was my grandfather's protégé. He was also my first coach in the Big Leagues for Boston in 1969. One of the gloves I still use (see Figure 0.3) is a Bobby Doerr MacGregor model circa 1940. Go figure, it was also the model my Aunt Annabelle favored. She played professional women's baseball, and that glove is in the Hall of Fame in Cooperstown in the "League of Their Own Display."

It's all connected. Today, Dave plays second base for my over-35 team, the Burlington Cardinals. He's out there in rain, sleet, or snow, and that one Sunday in August that is always hotter than Hades. He wants to play for us in the worst way, and sometimes he does … but even Bobby Doerr had a bad day.

Jericho, Vermont's Snowflake Bentley once said that no two snowflakes are the same. I believe no two gloves are the same, and paraphrasing Henry—not Bill—James: each one of them has a flaw, but it is its own flaw, not its neighbors. James said, "content yourself with the terrible algebra" of your own inadequacies. Good advice for a ballplayer.

The greatest, best defensive player I have ever seen mentally and physically is Ichiro Suzuki. As Dave writes in Chapter 2, all of his gloves were made by the master glovemaker Nobuyoshi Tsubota. On December 7, 1978 I was released by the Red Sox and deported to Quebec, Canada to play for the Montreal Expos. That season, spring training was just west of Daytona Beach (once I was also released by the Duval county jail—but that's another story, Dave …). The glove reps all show up the first week of February to try to sign players. MacGregor had gone belly up. I had had my fill of Wilson's product. A Mizuno motorhome pulled up at the ballpark gate. Who should emerge from that RV but Mr. Tsubota himself, and he made my very next glove, which I used until my last day in Major League Baseball. The very same Mr. Tsubota made all of Ichiro's gloves 40 years later. There is a connection through the glove.

Finally, why did I write this foreword? Because I'm a forward-thinking guy! Want to save baseball from itself? Everyone is saying how slow the game has become, and even some of the changes to the glove have been designed to speed up the game. The game is not slow, life is too fast. Too much multi-tasking, too much specialization. No one can make a decision, too much to think about, and no bullets in their guns.

In my sophomore year at USC, late in a game against Harvard in the spring, I was pitching to Pete Varney. Well, Pete had hit a home run off of me earlier in the game. I had the tying run on second base, so I decided to put Pete on first. You never put the winning run on first (unless it's Barry Bonds). My coach, Rod Dedeaux, came running, yelling, "Tiger! Tiger! What're ya' doing?"

I said, "Rod, I thought–"
"Stop it right there!" he said. "Cut your head off and let your body do the work!"

It's all about 27 outs and 9 innings. How do you do *that* quickly?

Throw strikes.
Keep the ball down.

Change speeds.
Be smooth.
Don't alibi.
And hustle.

That is what my dad wrote on my glove so many years ago, the Mike McCormick MacGregor model I still use some times. That glove helped me win more games than Satchell Paige, and as Casey Stengel says, "You could look it up!"

Defense is heroic; the glove is to a ballplayer what a six-shooter was to Josey Wales.

Right, Dave?
Right, Brooks?
Right, Ozzie?
Great book!

ACKNOWLEDGEMENTS

Babe Ruth once said, "The way a team plays as a whole determines its success. You may have the greatest bunch of individual stars in the world, but if they don't play together, the club won't be worth a dime." Babe was no poet—but when he was right, he was right. This book wouldn't be worth a dime without the team of people who contributed to its success.

I have received a great deal of support—intellectual, moral, and financial—from my colleagues at the University of Vermont. My good friend and co-director of the UVM Humanities Center, Luis Vivanco, encouraged me to write this book and inspired me to keep going when my efforts would flag. My friends in the Film and Television Studies Program, Deb Ellis, Todd McGowan, Hilary Neroni, Sarah Nilsen, and Hyon Joo Yoo, continue to champion my research and tolerate me writing about things far afield from our discipline. And for much of the final stages of writing this book, I was working as the Acting Dean of the Honors College. These colleagues, Brit Chase, Tina Griffis, Ian Grimmer, Martha Lance, Ann Kroll Lerner, Mariah Noth, and Camille Campanile, have been an extraordinary team and their professionalism and commitment to "good work" inspire me to do better each day. One of our teammates, Lily Fedorko, merits special thanks for formatting my bibliography and whipping my references into shape as the deadline for the manuscript loomed (the burger debt will be paid).

The College of Arts and Sciences (including Dean Bill Falls and Associate Dean John Burke) awarded me a Small Grant, whose name belies how huge was the chance it afforded to spend three days in Cooperstown doing archival research at the National Baseball Hall of Fame and Museum and to travel to Nocona, Texas to see a baseball glove factory and interview its owner. The Office of the Vice President for Research and the UVM Humanities Center helped sponsor my trip to Cuba and contributed to the cost of the camera that took many of the photographs in the book. Thanks to Richard Galbraith, Dan Harvey, and—once again—Luis for your generosity and indulgence.

Baseball is a game in which the history is always present, and in the course of writing this book, I have had the good fortune to talk with some of our finest baseball historians who helped me think through some thorny questions,

ACKNOWLEDGEMENTS xiii

confirm some nagging suspicions, and put me onto some unexpected sources. Conversations with John Thorn and Peter Morris proved invaluable in writing this book, as did the support of the archivists and staff of the Hall of Fame including Jim Gates, Tom Shieber, and Cassidy Lent. Above all, my friend, neighbor, and teammate, Tom Simon, founder of the Vermont Chapter of SABR and SABR's Deadball Era Committee, continues to be my best—and most fun—source of baseball history.

Although there are many sources on baseball cited in this book, a book about golf, Harry Brown's *The Golf Ball* (2015), served as a model for how to write a literate cultural life of a piece of sporting equipment and an inspiration that I could do the same. The entire production team at Routledge/Taylor and Francis has been a joy to work with. Sam Barbaro in New York oversaw the acquisition and development of the proposal, and her editorial assistants, Athena Bryan (in the book's first stages) and Erik Zimmerman (as the book neared the completion and permissions phase), were extraordinarily capable, patient, and efficient. My first job out of college was as an editorial assistant, and I very much appreciate the excellent work they did. In the UK, at Sunrise Setting, my copy editor, Sarah Cook, and her colleague Colin Read smoothed out the book's idiosyncrasies and showed remarkable tolerance toward a book about baseball.

This book would be severely impoverished without the wisdom and knowledge of a number of individuals who spoke to me about their relationship to the glove. Glovesmith Dave Katz and the Nokona company's Rob Storey were incredibly generous with their time and their knowledge. Throughout the book, I also quote the memories and reflections of players in the Vermont Men's Senior Baseball League. For the past six years, it has been my great pleasure to travel throughout the state to play baseball and meet players whose love of the game sustains them through middle age and beyond. Their stories enrich this book, and the opportunity to play with them has enriched my life in Vermont, my adoptive state. Of course, most of all, I would like to thank my teammates on the Burlington Cardinals who, every week, not only remind me why baseball is the greatest, most unpredictable game on earth, but also of the value and preciousness of friendship. You have no idea how much I value our summer Sundays, even when Patrick is challenging an umpire. No small part of the fun of playing with the Cardinals is getting to play behind Bill "Spaceman" Lee, who, in addition to being one of baseball's great characters and raconteurs—and still, at age 71, one hell of a ballplayer—is also a genuinely kind and generous man. As a kid who grew up in New England in the 1970s, I still sometimes can't believe I get to play ball with a guy who pitched game 7 for the Red Sox in the '75 World Series. But I really can't believe that he'd one day write a foreword to a book I had written. Thanks Bill!

Finally, of course, I am grateful to Lisa Brighenti, my wife, and our three children, Isaac, Anna, and Luke. When I think of the love and support you've given while writing this book and the joys we've shared throughout our lives on ballfields, on soccer fields, on mountain tops—and really, everywhere, I can't say it any better than Lou Ghehrig did—"I consider myself the luckiest man on the face of the earth."

INTRODUCTION

¿Segunda Base?: *Asking Questions about Baseball Gloves*

I do remember it, but I don't recall how I got it. I seemed to have always had it. It wouldn't surprise me if my dad got it for me when I was under a year old and threw it in my crib. It was a Paul Blair Wilson, very dark brown leather. I used it through about 3rd grade. It still lives at my parent's house.

Vermont Senior Men'sBaseball [VTMSBL] player,
Havana, Cuba. April, 2016

I am watching a baseball game at the Havana del Este park in Playa on the northern coast of Havana. The field is in view of the sea. A green concrete wall surrounds the park. Behind right center, there is a path that leads to the Max Borges, Jr.-designed Club Naútico, whose rolling, wave-shaped porticos, like Borges' iconic Tropicana club, are a vestige of the opulence of pre-revolution Cuba.

Beyond the wall, in between the field and the beach is a hardscrabble area of concrete and dry grass, an under-used play structure, and a handball court. My daughter, Anna, is playing on a team of Little Leaguers who have traveled to Cuba for a week of baseball coordinated in part by the Federación Cubana de Béisbol, the national organizing body for the sport. She is the only girl on the team.

During lulls in the action, my 9-year-old son Luke and I make our way to the handball court to play catch. I keep a watch on the game over the center field fence while lobbing balls off of the wall for my son to practice making game-saving grabs. Often, we are joined by other boys—never girls—who play catch and join Luke in the game of heroic wall-crashing despite not being able to exchange a word.

A few years before, I took a similar trip to the Dominican Republic, where my oldest son Isaac also played with a visiting team. In Puerto Plata, where he played, there was no telling who would show up at the field, let alone the location or condition of the fields where we'd play: Kids just off from school with their legs dangling over the walls ringing foul territory. Middle-aged men drinking Presidente beers, sometimes from well-appointed snack-bars, sometimes from makeshift stands. *Abuelas* with shopping bags offering critique, or encouragement, or just asking the score. Usually the fields would be carved out but still a part of the everyday life of the city, surrounded by shops, apartments, hospitals, and car mechanics. In one memorable game, however, we climbed into the foothills, and on the field in deep left stood a donkey, blithely chewing the outfield grass and beyond him, in thirty-foot letters composed of white stones lay a sign proclaiming "*Jesús Vive*"—Jesus Lives. Beyond that—the forest and the skies.

In Havana, things are more tightly controlled and not surprisingly, given the political context, lack the overt religious proselytizing if not the pomp and circumstance. Instead of traveling from field to field as we did in the DR, we play at Havana del Este each day, and whereas in the Dominican Republic, a game that was supposed to start at 2:00pm "*¡punto!*" could start as late as 4:00 or 6:00 or 8:00, in Cuba, a 2:00 game starts exactly at 2:00. Every day, after our mandatory cultural education experience, we arrive at Havana del Este—sharply—at 1:00 (see Figure 0.1), and there is no small seriousness about being let into the field through a locked gate each day. One gets the sense that the opposing fans, parents and friends of the young players, have been carefully vetted before arriving, and they are awaiting us well before we take our seats. The field is carefully maintained and festooned with red, white, and blue bunting to honor the American Little Leaguers. We would learn, during the first game, that the very same bunting—along with the Cuban flag unfurled at the games—had also ' graced the Cuban National baseball stadium for President Obama's visit to Havana only weeks before our trip. At first, there is little mingling of the American parents and the Cubans, but by the end of our stay, the adults have each migrated into the other side's seats, talking baseball and pointing out one another's children. Initially, I catch some quizzical looks—and consequently feel somewhat awkward—as the only adult leaving the stands to play catch with his son, but soon my mid-game routine becomes the norm, as do the other children joining our game and the eventual adults who stop to chat and express surprise and admiration that I am the father of *la niña* who hit a triple in the opening game.

In keeping with the official status accorded this visit by the Federación Cubana de Béisbol, at each of the games, officials for the Federación line the field keeping watch on the proceedings, introducing the players and the pre-game ceremonies, and sitting with the Americans. Although everyone attending is well-dressed for the games, the Federación representatives are easy to spot in the crowd with their khaki pants and polo shirts stretched tight across barrel chests. These are men who have played and coached baseball their entire lives at the highest level of a state-run development system. Baseball, for them, is intricately tied up with the Cuban government and their livelihoods, and it is a serious enterprise.

Figure 0.1 **Baseball gloves of youth players, Havana del Este park, Havana Cuba.** (*Source*: Photo by David Jenemann.)

Each day, as Luke and I make our way to the handball court where we play catch, we pass this group of big, athletic men intently watching the game. Typically, they pay no attention to me, a 40-something American and a 9-year-old boy, but one of the times as we pass, a voice behind me yells "*¡Oye! ¿Segunda Base?*"

I turn to the voice and am met by a solid, bald-headed figure with a thick black mustache. "*¿Segunda Base?*" he says again, pointing at me. "*¿Si . . . ?*" I say hesitatingly, not sure where this is going. I do, in fact play second base for an over-35 baseball team in my home town.

It must be my quizzical stare that causes him to do what he does next: He holds up his left hand and, spreading his fingers wide, uses his right hand to point at my left hand on which I am wearing my baseball glove. "*¡Segunda Base¡*" he says firmly.

"*Si . . . ¡Si!*" I say, finally understanding. "*¡Segunda Base!*"

What follows is a series of exchanges in broken English, even more broken Spanish, and pantomime, in which I convey that I play second base for an "old man" baseball team and that he, in addition to once being a second baseman is now the director of the under-19 baseball squad for the national development team. After the games that week, he grabs a glove and we go out onto the field to play catch with each other. Tree-trunk solid though he is now, my partner is every inch a second baseman. His footwork is impeccable as he receives my throws, and, shifting his weight with fluid speed, transfers the ball from his glove to his throwing hand to deliver it back to me in an instant. I play second base. He is a second baseman.

But how did he know that he and I shared this position in common, just by looking at my glove? The answer, as anyone who plays the game competitively past a certain age will likely know, is that my glove is 11.25 inches from the heel of its palm to the tip of the middle finger. It is obviously not a catcher's or first baseman's mitt, which, as "mitts" aren't gloves at all and don't have separated fingers. It is certainly not 12.75 inches long, which would mean I was an outfielder and—until recently—violating the official rules of baseball along with almost every other outfielder in the game (but more on that later). It is also not 12 inches long, with a closed webbing, which would likely mean I was a pitcher. It isn't even 11.5 or 11.75 inches, which probably would mark me as a shortstop or third baseman.

No, my glove is at least a quarter-inch shorter than any of those other gloves, which makes it the smallest glove on the field—but only by that quarter-inch.

This book is about that quarter-inch. More specifically it is about how that tiny amount of leather could tell a Cuban baseball coach a world of information about a Vermont professor, the common experiences we've shared, the ways our identities, our bodies, and perhaps even our perspectives on the world have been shaped by that quarter-inch.

It's fitting that this book appears in a series geared toward the "Creative Teaching and Learning in Anthropology," because this book is also, to a great extent, about how that Vermont professor taught himself about the discourses of anthropology through his experiences with an object he had never given much thought to, except when he dropped a fly ball.

The genesis of this project is—like most of my work—the result of a naïve question. I direct the University of Vermont Humanities Center with my friend and colleague Luis Vivanco, a cultural anthropologist who has co-written a successful introductory textbook to cultural anthropology (Welsch and Vivanco, 2015) and whose own work examines the history and uses of the bicycle across a variety of political, economic, and legal contexts (Vivanco, 2013).

Luis was telling me about his work, and this series of books on the cultural life of objects in which his bicycle research appeared. Luis had assumed the role as one of the series editors, and I was fascinated by the variety of objects the series dealt with. In addition to Luis' book on bicycles, there was a book on coffee (Tucker, 2011); one on alcohol (Chrzan, 2013); even one on the fabric Lycra (O'Connor, 2011). Each of these "anthropologies of stuff" examined their objects from different perspectives (activism and community development, globalization, corporate and industrial history), but each made the case for a compelling and intricate life behind the objects of our everyday existence. It was time to ask Luis my naïve question: "Who's doing your book about baseball gloves?"

"Why would we do a book about baseball gloves?" Luis asked in return.

I answered with an enthusiastic thumbnail sketch of why, for me, a baseball glove is the most interesting object in all of sports: Within the game, they have a fascinating history. Initially players didn't wear them. Then when they did start wearing them, they were reportedly teased for being sissies. They've changed remarkably from the early days when they didn't have fingers to what they are today. They're a standard piece of equipment for the game, and yet they're the most variable item on the field, differing in size, shape, color, and material depending on the position of the player, but also sometimes on factors like race or sense of style. And that's just on the field. Think of the way baseball gloves are passed from generation to generation, as well as the various rituals and traditions about how you break them in, how you treat them when not in use, how you store them in the winter, etc., each practice with an elaborate set of lore and received wisdom. Then there's the way the glove figures as a metaphor for all sorts ideas about what it means to be an American: Bruce Springsteen donning one in his video for "Glory Days;" Steve McQueen taking one in "the hole" in *The Great Escape*; Allie's glove in *Catcher in the Rye*. "But of course," I went on, "there's also the fact that despite all of the national cultural identity tied up in baseball, nearly all glove production has moved offshore . . . So there's a global economic story there as well."

"Why don't you write the book about the baseball glove, Dave?" Luis asked, after I finished my breathless discourse.

"But I'm not a cultural anthropologist, Luis," I protested. "I'm a film professor."

"But your work is in cultural theory," Luis responded, and you already know a lot of the discourses in the field—plus, you know baseball and baseball gloves. You've been essentially doing participant observation for years."

As I have often done throughout my professional career, I had stumbled into a potential project, but before I agreed to do it I wanted to be sure I was up to the task. "I could write a book about baseball, but what do I need to know in order to write a book about baseball gloves for anthropology students?" I asked.

"You have to ask questions," Luis replied. "It's the way we approached our cultural anthropology textbook. That's why we called it *Asking Questions*."

Asking questions—I could do that. After all, a question had gotten me into this. So I started asking questions about baseball gloves—of myself, of other players, of the historical record, and the question I started with was this one:

What is the first sensation that comes to mind when you think about a baseball glove?

Maybe it's the smell. There is something utterly distinctive about the smell of a baseball glove. Like "new car smell," or "Chinatown," a baseball glove is an amalgam of aromas combining together to produce a scent unlike anything else. Even though individual expressions of the form may vary (a Subaru smells different than a Porsche and Montreal's Chinatown is distinct from New York's or San Francisco's), there is nevertheless no mistaking the smell of a new car for the smell of Chinatown.

It is the same for a baseball glove. New, there is the odor of leather, and coupled with that is the smell of the tanning process that gives the leather its character. Each color of dye imparts a slightly different scent character. A black glove, a walnut glove, and a red glove will all smell slightly different. Perhaps, at the wrist strap there is the funk of lamb's wool and the slightly acrid, caustic tinge of new stitching in the embroidered label. The lettering, burned into the leather, imparts more notes.

But the smell of a new glove is like an opening movement when compared to the symphony of a broken-in and well-used glove—a sonnet compared to an epic poem. A well-worn glove still holds the memory of the new glove as an undertone, but it also holds the scent of infield clay and outfield grass. Depending on how it is broken in, an older glove will smell of glove oil, or neatsfoot oil, or Vaseline. Or maybe, alongside the grass and the dust, it will smell just slightly of shaving cream, of lanolin, of a parent or grandparent, who smelled something like that glove when they taught you to shave or when they sat close by your side and told you the mysteries of the game like they were revealing to you the meaning of the world.

And lastly, a well-worn glove will smell like sweat and salt. The lambswool and the padding and the leather itself will absorb the smell of the wearer, of the days in the sun spent playing and the nights on the couch spent pounding the pocket into just the right shape.

Or maybe the sensation you first experience is what a glove looks like. Again, a new glove and old present a different aesthetic. New, the leather fairly shines, its lacing and stitching, crisp, clean and true. Its label stands off from the leather like a billboard on a buff landscape—which is just what the label is—advertising to the world that the owner is partisan of Rawlings, with its classic sweeping white script on a red background. Then there are the aspirational "E's" for Easton, vectoring in three directions into infinity, or some players will sport the geometric "M's" and abstracted "runbird" distinctive to Mizuno, or maybe, depending on the player and the year, there is the profile—not unlike the face on the old buffalo nickel—of Comanche Chief Peta Nocona on the wrist of a Nokona ball glove.

As with the smell of a broken-in glove, the look of an older model is likewise distinctive. The pocket is darker where the sweat and the oil and a thousand caught balls combine, the tooled letters in the palm obliterated by endless pounding. The labels are faded and frayed. For some, the laces will be cracked and re-knotted; for others, there will be efforts at repair, sprucing up, and customization: New laces and cleaned leather, inked and painted sections, providing a player's glove with personality. This past summer, a teammate of mine arrived at a game with a glove he had bought on eBay. It was a basic, conservative Rawlings first basemen's mitt, walnut brown in color, but the previous owner had relaced the entire glove with baby blue laces. We both agreed it was one of the most beautiful things we had ever seen.

Sound, likewise, plays its part in the experience of a glove. A new glove gently creaks as you bend and fold it, the fibers of the leather straining as the owner tries to make it pliable. The thumb and pinky softly click—"tick, tick!"—together as you stiffly close your hand, trying to loosen the glove's hinges.

The sounds of a new glove are tentative and expectant, but soon, those sounds will be replaced by more assertive ones. The fingers will snap together with force and you'll hear the explosive pop of a baseball hitting the pocket of the glove. When people describe the sounds of a game of baseball, they often talk about "the crack of the bat" as though that is somehow unique to the game, but wooden bats and mallets strike balls in many sports. For me, the sound of a ball meeting a glove is truly unlike any sound in the world. In one of the interviews for the book, I traveled to Meriden, CT to speak to the "Glovesmith" Dave Katz, who breaks in gloves for people. As we spoke, Dave and I took turns pounding a ball into one of my gloves (see Figure 0.2). The audio file of our interview is punctuated with that sound just as surely as the written transcript is dotted with periods and commas.

Of course, for you, the sense of touch might be the first thing you experience. The stiffness of a new glove fights against the tendons of your hands and fingers. It is frankly uncomfortable to try on a new glove. The leather is slick and unnatural, and you have to contort your hand into a stiffened claw to put your fingers in their stalls—the space for your fingers to rest while waiting for

Figure 0.2 **Gloves for sale by "Glovesmith" Dave Katz (2017), Meriden, CT.** (*Source*: Photo by David Jenemann.)

action. Broken in, the feel of a glove is something else altogether. It fits—well, not really like a glove, not these days, but more on that later. Rather, a well-worn glove feels more like a hammer in the hand, a tool exquisitely designed to do a certain job (catching a 9-inch circumference sphere), and the increasing suppleness of the leather as it breaks in only enhances the efficiency with which it accomplishes that task.

Finally, lest you think you are forgotten—although I can't imagine there are many people for whom this the primary sensation of the glove—a glove has a taste. Watch a game at any level: Little Leaguers will be distractedly gnawing on their laces, while older players will use their teeth to tighten them so as to not have to take the glove off of their hands while in the field. Here, as with the other senses, the taste of the glove—of leather and sunshine and dust—is all its own.

All of this is to say that a baseball glove is a profoundly material object, appealing to all of the senses, and no account of a baseball glove's cultural significance can—or should—ignore that materiality. As we will see, the material facts of a baseball glove's existence come into being as the result of a set of historical and cultural processes. The transformation of a piece of raw material, generally—although not exclusively—a piece of leather made from tanned steerhide, into a consumer product suited to playing the game of baseball seems like a relatively straightforward, even inevitable, process. But when considered in light of the history of the game, of changing ideas about gender, masculinity, race, and national identity, of evolving concepts of fair play, and of a transforming global economy, we can see that the material fact of a baseball glove is neither straightforward nor is it inevitable.

In an essay titled "My Glove: A Biography," sportswriter Stefan Fatsis describes the smell of his glove. It consists of "dirt, grass, saliva, sun, spring, childhood, summer, hope, skill, anticipation, achievement, fulfillment, memory, love, joy" (Fatsis, 2008: 17). What's significant about Fatsis' description is the way it evolves from concrete material impressions ("dirt, grass, saliva") to abstract ideas ("memory, love, joy"). Fatsis is on to something: At the same time that gloves have a material existence—what some people might call their ontology—they also participate in a whole range of activities that contribute to what we think about them at a given historical moment or at a significant juncture in our own life story. We call that aspect of a glove its *meaning*. Those meanings have changed historically as the glove has evolved materially. This is a book about baseball gloves, their history, their design, the way they're used, the cultural practices in which they feature. The early, inconspicuous, uniform color leather palm that served as the earliest catcher's glove of the 1870s and 1880s does and means something different than Boston Red Sox outfielder Mookie Betts' 2017 cherry red, black, and white-striped, 12.75-inch Wilson A2K model, which is made from both leather and Wilson's patented "Superskin" synthetic fiber.

This is also a book about how baseball gloves come to *mean* something for people in various contexts. That meaning is often unique to the individual. More
than perhaps any other piece of sports equipment, a baseball glove speaks to a
player's history, their family, and a sense of place (Selcraig, 2001). The glove I
played with as a 10-year-old, when all the world was full of possibility signifies
something very different to me than the glove I use now to coach my children
and play with my middle-aged teammates. A 2015 *New York Times* article attests
to the individuality inscribed in the baseball glove:

> Baseball players can choose what spikes they wear, what batting gloves they
> use and what bats they swing, but no matter their position, there is nothing
> more personal, more tailored to their own hand than the glove they take
> out on the field.

(Witz, 2015)

If a baseball glove is a uniquely personal item, it is also an item with more
wide-ranging cultural significance. Babe Ruth once claimed, "I won't be happy
until we have every boy in America between the ages of six and sixteen wearing
a glove and swinging a bat" (National Baseball Hall of Fame, 2013: 34), and
throughout much of the twentieth century, Ruth's dream was a reality for much
of the American populace. The baseball glove is a ubiquitous item in many
households in the United States, and as one of the iconic pieces of equipment
of "The National Pastime," the glove also came to stand for a series of ideas
about what it means to be an American. But the glove has also come to have
special significance for other, non-US cultures where baseball success functions
as a point of athletic *and* of national pride. In some cases that pride has a political dimension. As the historian of Japanese Baseball Yuko Kusaka tells us, "The
military suppressed playing baseball during the Second World War. After the
war, however, young people soon began to play the game in the ruins. Gloves
made of the skin of fishes were sold like hot cakes" (Kusaka, 1987: 272). In
other cases, donning the glove and claiming baseball for one's own country also
means claiming certain gender norms. "To the average Dominican, baseball is
a major source of cultural pride," *Sugarball* author Alan Klein writes, "When
you're born, the hospital puts a pink ribbon in your crib if you're a girl, and a
baseball glove if you're a boy" (Klein, 1991: 1).

So—another question: how and why does it come to pass that an object as
commonplace as a baseball glove comes to signify so much in a given cultural
context? It is fortuitous that Fatsis subtitles his essay "A Biography," for when
cultural anthropologists study the stuff of our everyday material existence, they
often, following an influential essay by Igor Kopytoff (1986) refer to their work

in terms of a "biography of a thing." As in the best biographies of historical individuals, biographies of things have to take into account the whole range of forces that contribute to a life story: where it comes from and where it ends up, the people it interacts with and the stories it takes part in. "In doing the biography of a thing," Kopytoff explains . . .

> [O]ne would ask questions similar to those one asks about people: What, sociologically, are the biographical possibilities inherent in its "status" and in the period and culture, and how are these possibilities realized? Where does the thing come from and who made it? What has been its career so far, and what do people consider to be an ideal career for such things? What are the recognized "ages" or periods in the thing's "life," and what are the cultural markers for them? How does the thing's use change with its age, and what happens to it when it reaches the end of its usefulness?

> (Kopytoff, 1986: 66)

But what form should that biography take? Kopytoff's work appears in a collection of essays edited by Arjun Appadurai called *The Social Life of Things* (1986). In his introduction to the collection, Appadurai announces that the objects of material culture, many of which also have lives as commodities in a system of exchange, are fundamentally interesting to anthropologists because they speak to so many different subfields of the discipline, and their meanings derive from that variation. As such, there are many different "biographies" of things, depending on the perspective of the anthropologist/biographer.

> Commodities, and things in general, are of independent interest to several kinds of anthropology. They constitute the first principles and the last resort of archaeologists. They are the stuff of "material culture," which unites archaeologists with several kinds of cultural anthropologists. As valuables, they are at the heart of economic anthropology and, not least, as the medium of gifting, they are the heart of exchange theory and social anthropology generally.

> (Appadurai, 1986: 5)

In the 30 years following Appadurai's collection and Kopytoff's influential essay, there has been an explosion of scholarship regarding the cultural life of objects (Berger, 2009; Lemonnier, 2012; Stewart, 1993; Woodward, 2007). Perhaps the most influential figure in this field is the British anthropologist Daniel Miller, who has spent much of the last three decades examining the daily life of stuff (Miller, 1987, 2005, 2010). If the stereotypical image of anthropologist is the figure out in the field who collects artefacts from some remote tribe or records the use of objects in an obscure religious practice (which, to be sure, is what some anthropologists do—and did), Miller made the case that there is a rich body of insight to be gained from studying how people use objects much closer to home in our own cultural back yards. If the constant refrain is that we in Western industrialized nations live in materialistic societies, Miller argues, shouldn't we be interested in how the materials of our everyday lives shape our habits and practices, how stuff takes on meaning and gives us meaning in return? We live in a world with "an endless proliferation of artefacts," Miller said (Miller, 2005: 4), but we should not lose sight that the sheer (literal) weight of all of the stuff produced in the world also carries the hefty cultural weight of meaning as well:

> An anthropological volume devoted to materiality should not ignore this colloquial usage [of materialism] and I will, for this reason, start this investigation with a theory of the most obvious and most mundane expression of what the term material might convey—artefacts. But this soon breaks down as we move on to consider the large compass of materiality, the ephemeral, the imaginary, the biological and the theoretical; all that which would have been external to the simple definition of an artefact. So the second theory of materiality to be introduced here will be the most encompassing, and will situate material culture within a larger conceptualisation of culture.
>
> (Miller, 2005: 4)

I find Miller's method compelling, for much the same reason I like Stefan Fatsis' "biography" of his glove. Both move from the raw material fact of the object to the panoply of associations that material existence evokes. A baseball glove is a piece of leather designed to perform a fairly inconsequential task (catching a baseball) and sold as a commodity that emerges out of and circulates in a multi-million dollar sporting goods industry. Between 2007 and 2014, for example, approximately 36 million baseball gloves were sold in the United States, at a *wholesale* cost of $1.05 billion.[1] A baseball glove is a decidedly materialist object—it's an expensive piece of equipment for a leisure activity—made (predominantly) in far-flung locations for people who generally live in another country. But in its materiality, it is also decidedly part of the larger conceptualization of culture.

Which culture is of course another question. Although baseball is played throughout the world, for the most part in this book I look at the way that the material existence of the glove—its design and evolution, the way it is made and shaped—gives way to broader questions of meaning and significance in the United States.

This movement from material to meaning seems like a fitting way to look at the baseball glove given the development of the cultural anthropology of stuff as a discipline, but as I said, I am not an "anthropologist". I generally consider myself a cultural historian, and I prefer to do my research poring through archives, looking at old photographs, and reading old newspapers to find out how we got to now. Fortunately, this type of historical analysis is common to cultural anthropologists and poststructuralist theorists in the humanities and social sciences who tend to eschew the cause-and-effect chain of narrative history, and instead look at the fluid, evolving "practice of everyday life" (Certeau, 1984) as a function of a variety of phenomena, beliefs, and cultural practices evident at a given historical moment. This type of historical analysis develops during the latter part of the twentieth century in the work of such influential writers like Michel Foucault, Fernand Braudel, Judith Butler, Theodor Adorno, Frantz Fanon, and Pierre Bourdieu, each of whom were influenced to a greater or lesser extent by the works of Karl Marx and Sigmund Freud and the notion that the prevailing forces of certain cultural beliefs and practices helped materially shape historical events.

While these writers can hardly be considered to be in intellectual agreement on all fronts—indeed, they were often at odds with and quite critical of one another—what they share is a sense that history is a set of competing practices and performances spread out unevenly over the whole of society rather than the work of a handful of what Hegel called World-Historical Individuals moving the world to its idealistic ends (Hegel and Hoffmeister, 1975). For his part, the French historian Michel Foucault deemed the task of historical analysis analogous to archaeology, but not archaeology in the sense of reconstructing the fossil record or historical timeline to "rediscover the continuous, insensible transition" relating one idea "on a gentle slope, to what precedes them, surrounds them, or follows "them". Instead, the archaeological work of a historian is invested in reconstructing discourses, "the thoughts, representations, images, themes, preoccupations" that are prevalent at a given historical moment. Foucault saw these discourses "as practices obeying certain rules"—rules that had real, material consequences not only for individuals' beliefs but how their bodies interacted in the world (Foucault, 2002: 155).

Foucault's contemporary, the French sociologist Pierre Bourdieu (1984, 1990), whose work profoundly influences cultural anthropology, referred to the way individuals embodied the cultural practices and beliefs of their historical epoch and in turn shaped history through their use of material goods; a culture's "habitus." For Bourdieu, history is never simply the will of a handful of individuals acting out their interests. Instead, "the source of historical action," Bourdieu explains, is not an active subject confronting society as if that society were an object constituted externally. This source resides neither in consciousness nor in things but in the relation between two states of the social, that is, between the history objectified in things, in the form of institutions, and the history incarnated in bodies, in the form of that system of enduring dispositions that I call habitus. The body is in the social world but the social world is also in the body.

(Bourdieu, 1990: 190)

"History objectified in things." This is the story I would like to tell about the baseball glove, a history not of individual invention and ingenuity on the part of "the first person to wear a baseball glove," but instead a story of competing myths, ideas and beliefs embodied by the material existence of the baseball glove as it inserts itself into the cultural practice of baseball. And so, in Chapter 1 of the book, I spend some time looking at moments in the historical evolution of the glove that point us to how the glove is used today. The brilliant French medievalist, Jacques Le Goff, whose work straddles the line between history and anthropology, believed that historical periods had two sides. On the one hand was the material reality of historical events, on the other was what people believed about those events, imagination, and dreams (Le Goff, 1988). The cultural history of the baseball glove bears the hallmarks of those two realities. On the one hand, the glove is a material object that comes into existence in a certain time and place and for a certain purpose, on the other, it is a bearer of a set of beliefs—about fair play, about sportsmanship, about what it meant— and means—to be a man. Throughout this book we will have cause to return to the questions of the glove's material existence and its meaning in contemporary contexts using the tools of cultural anthropology, but my aim in the first chapter is to try to tell some of the competing of versions of the story of the glove at a few key moments in its evolution by using the tools of historical research: archive visits, original documents, correspondences, press clippings, personal memories, and images.

Of course, to do any research on baseball, one knows where to travel, at least initially, and so I drove from Burlington, Vermont to Cooperstown, New York to spend time in the Archives at the Giamatti Research Center at the National Baseball Hall of Fame and Museum. The Hall and the Research Center are pilgrimage sites for fans and historians of the game, and working with the archival record a story of the glove emerged far different than the one typically presented. Some of these are primary sources, some are secondary. Oftentimes, these sources contradict one another, reflecting as they do the beliefs of the person offering the source as authoritative. Taken together, these sources help paint a picture—albeit certainly not the only one—of what a historical anthropology of a baseball glove might look like. And that story runs parallel to and at times contradicts the standard commonly accepted accounts of the adoption of the glove.

But my goal in writing from this perspective is not to produce a straightforward chronological history. In fact, that story has been told—and quite engagingly—by a number of historians of the game including Peter Morris, whose *Game of Inches* (Morris, 2010), reveals the intricate and incremental development of all facets of the game, including the glove. Likewise, Steve Rushin's lovely *The 34-Ton Bat* (Rushin, 2013) tells the history of the game through objects ranging from bobble heads to jock straps—and of course the baseball glove. Finally, Noah Liberman, in his colorful 2003 book *Glove Affairs: The Romance, History and Tradition of the Baseball Glove* (Liberman, 2003) gives an extensive overview of how the glove developed in the professional game and how major league players have adopted—and adapted to—the glove. I turn to Liberman, Rushin and other historians throughout the book to provide insight into how ideas about the glove evolved. But since the standard history of the baseball glove has been well told, instead in what follows, I look first at some of the competing discourses surrounding the origins of the glove and how those discourses reflect both beliefs about the game and beliefs about masculinity. These competing discourses ultimately get absorbed by the adoption of the glove in the official rules and the marketing of the glove as a consumer good.

As Igor Kopytoff reminds us, what interests anthropologists in the "biography" of a material object is both how the object is introduced into culture and how that introduction changes the culture and the object simultaneously. "Biographies of things can make salient what might otherwise remain obscure," Kopytoff claims. "What is significant about the adoption of alien objects—as of alien ideas—is not the fact that they are adopted, but the way they are culturally redefined and put to use" (Kopytoff, 1986: 67). While I start with adoptions—the origin of the glove and how it entered the game—from those origins, I turn my attention to certain moments in the history of the glove that reveal what some of the prevailing cultural practices and preoccupations are in the glove's history—how, as Kopytoff says, it is being redefined and put to use: the debate about whether gloves should be left in the field between innings in the 1950s; and the debates about the appropriate size of the glove that re-emerge once every generation or so. Both of these moments, while briefly sketched, will ultimately be rejoined and amplified in later chapters when I turn my attention more directly to questions of materiality and meaning. In this section, I am not so much trying to tell a straightforward chronological story of the glove's development as much as I try to understand some of the cultural forces at play in the glove's introduction and adoption. The typical version of how the glove made its way into the game of baseball involves tales of how the first players who used them were ridiculed as unmanly, sissies, or worse (Liberman, 2003). From this perspective, the glove is intimately connected to notions of gender and sexuality, but after extensive research into the history of the glove, what I found was that if this was *a* story common to the introduction of the glove, it was by no means the only story. Indeed, competing discourses about performance in the field, commerce, and safety may well have been more compelling counter-narratives that trumped any ridicule players might have faced.

But these historical questions tend to lead directly to material ones: Once the glove is introduced and accepted, how does it arrive at the form we now know? What are the forces that shape the glove, and how does the evolution of the glove shape the game and its players? These are also questions with an anthropological underpinning, and the focus of my second chapter where I turn more directly to the material life of the glove by examining the evolution of its design and the way it is made and shaped today. The anthropologist Tim Ingold describes the evolution of a material object as an "hylomorphic" process in which "form-givers," inventors, designers, and innovators take raw material and give it shape. This process is one fraught with tensions and contradictions. "To create any thing, Aristotle reasoned, you have to bring together form (morphe) and matter (hyle). In the subsequent history of Western thought, this hylomorphic model of creation became ever more deeply embedded." Ingold argues that this process of creation is inherently unstable. Giving material form is an essentially authoritarian gesture. Not only is the form-giver putting his or her stamp on indeterminate nature, but form-giving also announces to others that an idea about the proper comportment of material reality takes precedence over others. "Form came to be seen as imposed by an agent with a particular design in mind, while matter, thus rendered passive and inert, became that which was imposed upon" (Ingold, 2010: 92). On the other hand, for Ingold and other theorists (Wark, 2017; Coleman, 2010) the process of design innovation can also be an inherently individual and radical act—giving new life to the dead material ossified in their previous forms. "Form," Ingold argues,

is death; form-giving is life . . . [I]t is a question not of imposing preconceived forms on inert matter but of intervening in the fields of force and currents of material wherein forms are generated. Practitioners, I contend, are wanderers, wayfarers, whose skill lies in their ability to find the grain of the world's becoming and to follow its course while bending it to their evolving purpose.

(Ingold, 2010: 91)

The original innovators of the glove—players cutting off the fingers or sewing the fingers together of pre-existing gloves, stuffing them with grass, or wool, or meat to enhance their padding—these were the type of figures giving life to the material world Ingold valorizes, but so too are the professional designers, manufacturers, and "glove doctors," who come after them and make—and remake—the glove into the form we know today.

In Chapter 2, I pick up the historical threads from Chapter 1 and use them to consider how the material evolution of the baseball glove's design, manufacture, and breaking-in is interwoven with the evolution of the rules of the game. A baseball glove starts its life as a piece of leather, is manufactured as part of a multi-billion-dollar sporting goods industry, and is sold—or given—to a player. From there a number of things happen to it. First, most gloves need to be broken-in, and that breaking-in process is arguably one of the most contested practices in all of sports. So vexed is the set of beliefs about how to break in a glove, that a small group of professional glove gurus, glove doctors, and glovesmiths have made their careers around reshaping the glove for the use of others. I am conscientious about the fact that the discipline of anthropology has long moved past its stereotypical and exoticizing preoccupation with shamans and "witch doctors." Nevertheless, part of the appeal of baseball as an object of anthropological practice in general and of the glove in particular is that superstition, ritual, and myth is so deeply intertwined with the history of the game, and the fact that there is a culture of "glove doctors" which has developed to see into the mystery of the glove is one of the endearing features of this project. As players adopt and adapt the equipment, a series of discourses help illuminate how the glove functions as part of the broader practice of the game. That design evolution has profound impacts on how players play, and, following the theories of anthropologists and design theorists, I consider the idea that the glove shapes the player as much as the player shapes the glove.

One of the happy discoveries of this book is the number of fascinating makers and shapers who have contributed to the evolution of the glove. From early innovators like Albert Goodwill Spalding and Arthur "Foxy" Irwin, who each lay (tenuous) claims to introducing the glove, to the pitcher Bill Doak, who patented the glove's webbing, players have made significant contributions to the life of the glove. Then there are the family dynasties whose multigenerational commitment to the glove have helped craft this story. The famous father and son glove designers Harry and Rollie Latina, who, working for Rawlings for nearly half a century held dozens of patents, and their innovative designs are still in use today. The Storey family of Nocona, Texas ran a small sporting-goods company who started making ball gloves in 1934. Today, the founder's grandson Rob Storey is still the Executive Vice President of the company and still makes ball gloves, and the Nokona company is the last major manufacturer of baseball gloves left in the United States (Mayeda, 2017). Finally, there are the glove masters, doctors, and gurus. Some of them, like Mizuno's Nobuyoshi Tsubota who individually hand-crafted every one of Ichiro Suzuki's gloves (Lefton, 2008), and Wilson's Shigeaki Aso, the "Jedi Master" of gloves have assumed near legendary status—aided no doubt by US stereotypes about Asian masters of mystic arts. Other glove whisperers, like "Glovesmith" Dave Katz from Meriden, CT or Mike Wilkinson, the "Glove Doctor" from Vienna, OH, run small operations single-mindedly dedicated to one thing: breaking-in baseball gloves.

The subtitle of this book was originally supposed to be "From Flesh to Gold." This phrase was meant to reflect that, for many people, a glove goes from being a humble object made out of leather (the flesh) to an extremely significant bearer of value (the gold). Not only is there the fact that Rawlings offers the Gold Glove Award to the MLB players deemed the best fielders each year, but, in many respects gloves stand as signifiers for financial status, class, and race. In impoverished areas of the United States, and in countries like Cuba, Venezuela, the Dominican Republic and other parts of the Americas, players fashion gloves out of cardboard boxes, milk cartons, and duct tape, or they depend on mass donations of used and surplus gloves to feed their baseball dreams. In the United States, the cost of a new glove is one of the barriers to African Americans taking up the game (Brown and Bennett, 2015). On the other hand, in affluent corners of the world, parents often pay over $500 to outfit their sons or daughters—or themselves—in a model worn and endorsed by their favorite players. The glove can serve as a marker of class, wealth and excess. Billy Crystal once paid $239,000 for Mickey Mantle's glove; Hermès markets a $14,000 calf-skin model. At the same time however, gloves also have a personal significance that transcends monetary value. I have spoken to hundreds of people about their baseball gloves, and a repeated refrain is that their glove is priceless because of the memories it holds. "I will always own a ball glove," a player told me. "As long as I have two working arms and hands there will always be a ball glove in my house."

Thus, in Chapter 3, I look at how the questions I have been examining about the historical and material development of the glove coalesce around questions of meaning. How does a glove come to mean something for different individuals and groups? How does a glove come to signify a range of ideas about national identity, or gender, or race? How does it take on value? Sometimes those meanings fit within theoretical categories, at other times, those meanings are idiosyncratic. In this chapter, I try to balance the deterministic theories of meaning with the individual expressions I have seen in a variety of contexts.

This balancing act leads me to one of the fundamental challenges I had writing this book. As someone who works in cultural theory and cultural history, I am in my comfort zone when I'm working with texts. Although one can successfully do cultural anthropology by focusing solely on document analysis and archival evidence, the work of many cultural anthropologists involves going into the field, doing first-hand observations of behaviors and languages, conducting interviews with informants, and—where appropriate—participating in the cultural practices they wish to study. In short, to think like an anthropologist, I had to get out of the archives and into the field. So, as I proceed in Chapters 2 and 3 of the book, I extend my examination of the historical development of the baseball glove into questions of material and meaning as they're experienced today. As with the histories of baseball gloves that inspired me and marked my path, in terms of a fieldwork centered on baseball, I have also had good models. Beginning in the 1970s, the Union College anthropology professor George Gmelch has been writing about the rituals, beliefs and magic of baseball. Gmelch's work on the anthropology of baseball is so compelling, in part, because for a number of years, as a young man, he played baseball professionally, and then as a professor of anthropology, he returned to the game as an ethnographer, interviewing players, coaches, fans, and families about their experiences and beliefs and observing the set of practices and rituals associated with the game as played on the field and lived throughout minor and major league seasons. "Why would an anthropologist want to study baseball?" Gmelch asks:

> That was often the first question reporters asked me after the publication of *Inside pitch: Life in professional baseball* a book based on several seasons of fieldwork riding buses and hanging out with ballplayers. The short answer was that since sport is a product of culture – and anthropology is interested in all aspects of culture – why not study baseball?

> (Gmelch, 2008: 10)

What Gmelch discovered is that baseball bears a lot of the hallmarks of any other culture an anthropologist could study: rituals and magic practices, subcultures and linguistic idiosyncracies, and from this he produced a rich ethnography of the game as lived by those who play and follow the game.

Likewise, my colleague at the University of Vermont, Ben Eastman, did extensive fieldwork in Cuba, examining the way baseball is woven into the fabric of post-revolutionary Cuba, interviewing teams, observing games, doing extensive research in news sources and government statistics, and braving the intense debates about baseball in the "Hot Corner" of Havana's *Parque Central*. What he discovered was the way that baseball had been remade in the years after the Revolution from a "conduit of capitalism to scepter of socialism" with baseball as the centerpiece of a mass socialist sports program. "In the wake of the revolution baseball was no longer *a* battlefield, but '*the* battlefield for working out the differences' between Cuba and the United States" (Eastman et al., 2013) For both Gmelch and Eastman, baseball has proven a rich terrain for anthropological research and observation.

In the spirit of trying to think like an anthropologist and to use the glove as a practical teaching tool for students interested in the discipline, I do think it's important to report "from the field" as it were about the way various populations interact with gloves and the practices and beliefs that arise around them in given circumstances. I have not done anything quite so ambitious as traveling with professional ball clubs over the course of five seasons, nor have I done extensive research in Cuba—and I'm certainly not as courageous as Ben was to brave the "hot corner," in Havana, but like Gmelch, I have returned to the game and to the glove in a variety of capacities as I enter my middle age, and like Eastman, I have traveled to Latin America to see how the game is played and understood by everyday players and fans. For the past six years, I have been playing baseball with an over-35 Men's Senior Baseball League team in Burlington, Vermont. From late April through late September, almost every Sunday afternoon, you can find me on a ballfield, playing baseball throughout the state of Vermont with former high school and college players and a scattering of former pros. Our "old man" baseball is a hard ball, wood bat league, and after six seasons, I have had the opportunity to see first-hand how this population of players interacts with their gloves, buys them, breaks them in, gives them to their children, inherits them from their parents, and—most importantly—uses them in the field. These men, approximately 200 of them, are the primary population I've observed and interviewed, and throughout the book their thoughts about the glove as an object of significance informs how I've written about the baseball glove. Vermont is a small, relatively homogeneous state, and I have no illusions about the fact that these men provide a universal picture of what the gloves mean to all populations. First of all, they're all men, and they're predominately white, and throughout the book, I try to remind the reader—and myself—that the glove likely means something different in different contexts, and different cultural situations. Nevertheless, what these men had to tell me about how their gloves took on meaning for them felt "right" within a specific cultural context, so I include their words and their observations as a way of acknowledging a certain cultural constellation into which the glove fits.

Further, in addition to traveling to Cooperstown, Cuba, and the Dominican Republic (as well as Montpelier, Randolph, and Chelsea, Vermont), I have had the good fortune of interviewing the Executive Vice President and grandson of the founder of Nokona, Rob Storey in Texas, and the "Glovesmith" Dave Katz in Connecticut. In many ways, these two men couldn't have been more different. Rob is a Texas businessman, and, it turns out, a Donald Trump supporter, at least insofar as he thinks he'll be good for business—although I didn't discover that until I read it in an article (Mayeda, 2017). Dave is a solo operation, Jewish, and has anti-Trump cartoons on his walls in amongst his photographs of Mickey Mantle. ("I've never lost a sale because of it. Nobody said, 'I don't like your political views, I'm leaving'."). Despite their differences, both men have dedicated their professional lives—and owe their livelihoods—to the baseball glove, and both were gregarious, engaging, knowledgeable, and kind as I peppered them with questions. I talked to each man for hours, had lunch at a Mexican restaurant with Rob, played catch with Dave. Their takes on the significance of the baseball glove and why they do what they do so complemented and amplified each other, that I have dedicated a section of the book to letting them speak for themselves as a way both of illustrating how a glove could mean so much to an individual and of revealing how this object cuts across much of the geographical and political divide in this country.

A couple of notes about the structure of the book: As I mentioned, some of the questions were the typical ones writers ask about a topic: "What's been written about baseball gloves?" (quite a lot, it turns out). "Where would I go to learn more about them?" (some places nearby, like local ballfields; some far away, like Nocona, Texas). But some of the questions I needed to ask dealt with how I could think like an anthropologist while writing this book. There is a baseball analogy here: I am not a naturally gifted baseball player. When I returned to the game after many years, I had to train myself to be proficient so that I wouldn't embarrass myself if front of my teammates. After a number of years, I consider myself a reliable ballplayer, not great but solid. The thing is, I had to practice. The same holds true with me writing this book from the perspective of the field of anthropology. I had to practice the discipline. In the spirit of writing a book about anthropology for students who likewise are learning the discipline, throughout the book I have included break-out sections in which I invite readers to practice being an anthropologist, the way I had to practice being one when writing the book. These are not meant to provide the depth and breadth of a methods course in anthropology. Instead, these "practicing anthropology" sections are designed to give students an opportunity to think like an anthropologist when dealing with an object like a baseball glove. The first of them appears on the next page (see Breakout Box 0.1).

A second thing to note about what to expect from this book: part of the pleasure I find in doing research is discovering the anomalous and unexpected, the stories that illuminate the texture and character of a historical period as much as the chronological facts. Throughout the book, I have included a number of episodes in the life of the glove that point the way to the larger cultural issues embodied in its cultural uses and practices. I call these sections "signposts," and they are stories in the history of the glove that would otherwise seem innocuous, but which help explain something about its historical, material, and

Breakout Box 0.1:   Practicing Anthropology: Fieldwork and Interviews

Much of the work of being an anthropologist involves qualitative social science research methods like participant observation, interviews, and site visits. Each of those methods has developed throughout the history of the fields of anthropology and sociology to reflect best practices in the discipline as well as an acknowledgement that working with human subjects in the field has an ethical dimension and that social scientists have sometimes not acted in the best interest of their subjects (Lenza, 2004; AAA, 2012). If you are reading this book in an anthropology course, you likely know about or are learning those methods.

As I mentioned, as a cultural theorist and not a cultural anthropologist, I was not accustomed to conducting interviews for my work, and so I had

Figure 0.3 **The Burlington Cardinals (including "Spaceman" Bill Lee with his glove) on the bench** (*Source*: Photo by Gordon Miller.)

to learn about the principles and practices of participant observation and ethnographic interviews. Fortunately, here, as throughout the book, I had my friend Luis Vivanco to help give me advice. In his *Cultural Anthropology* textbook, he and his colleague Robert Welsch write:

> Participant observation gives us many insights about how social life in another society is organized, but it is up to us as anthropologists to find systematic evidence for our perceptions. So another key goal of fieldwork is to flesh out our insights and gain new perspectives from interviews, or systematic conversations with informants, to collect data.

> (Welsch and Vivanco, 2016: 64)

Luis includes a handy chart for how to think systematically about interviews. Other authors (Spradley, 1979; Okely, 2011) give extensive guidance on how to conduct interviews. However, conducting the research for this book, I was at first hardly systematic. In addition to spending a lot of time on the bench, on the field, and in sporting goods stores, I conducted a number of informal and formal interviews, both structured and unstructured. For instance, my conversations with Rob Storey and Dave Katz were scheduled but long and free-ranging (although I knew there were a couple of questions I had to ask each of them). They produced over 30 pages of typescript—each! and my conversations with other players were informal—and at times observational, but a baseball field is hardly an easy place to take notes, especially when you're playing second base.

However, when it came time to formally questioning my fellow VTMSBL players, I was able to boil my approach down to four relatively concise questions:

1. What do you remember about your first glove? How did you get it? Do you still have it?
2. How do you break in a glove?
3. What glove do you wear now? Why? How long have you had it? How did you get it?
4. Are there any noteworthy stories regarding a glove or fielding you remember or would like to share?

As an assignment ask your students to do some participant observation at a variety of sites. They can watch or maybe even play in a baseball game: How are baseball gloves utilized? What types of gloves do players use? How does this change at various levels of the game? Can students use observation/ fieldwork skills to address questions of utility? They can also visit sporting goods stores and antique and second-hand stores. How are gloves sold? How is a story of value created by a glove's placement in the store? How does that story change if the glove is designated as second-hand? As antique?

Next, your students can interview subjects and practice field interviews. Have your students arrange to interview someone with a baseball glove. Why do people play with the glove they do? Why do parents purchase a particular glove for their children? How much did they spend? How do they use their gloves? What stories do they tell about their gloves? Although a baseball glove might seem a low-stakes subject for ethnographic interviews, interviewing subjects about their practices and beliefs surrounding a base-ball glove can be both a rewarding and instructive pedagogical experience.

Suggested Reading

Okely, Judith. *Anthropological Practice: Fieldwork and the Ethnographic Method.* Oxford: Berg Publishers, 2011.

Spradley, J. *The Ethnographic Interview.* New York: Holt, Rinehart and Winston, 1979.

Welsch, R.L. and Vivanco, L.A. *Asking Questions about Cultural Anthropology: A Concise Introduction.* New York: Oxford University Press, 2016.

cultural existence. At the end of the first two chapters, I include a couple of these signposts both to point up some of the idiosyncrasies of the game and to gesture to some of the issues that will underpin the next chapter. Hence, the ongoing debate over the length of the glove foreshadows the relationship between the rules and design, and Mizuno's van tour of the United States in the 1970s to entice American professional players can be seen as a harbinger of the globalization of the glove industry in the following decades. My first signpost, briefly, is the story of Arthur "Foxy" Irwin:

Not many baseball fans know the name of Arthur Alexander Irwin, but per-haps they should.[2] Irwin, who was born in Canada, was a shortstop and coach in the wild, early days of Major League Baseball, when teams were still very much in flux. Although he ended his playing career in 1894 with the Philadelphia Phillies and managed for the Phillies, Washington Senators and New York Giants, he was also associated with such teams as the Worcester Worcesters, the Providence Grays, and the Philadelphia Quakers, all of which played—and folded—in the 1880s and 1890s.

Irwin had a remarkable baseball career. He is widely credited with introduc-ing the fielder's glove to the game in 1883 after he sewed the ring and middle fingers of a buckskin horse driver's glove together to protect his own two broken fingers and accommodate the bandages. The glove caught on, and within a year Irwin, with an entrepreneurial zeal that would characterize much of his life, started marketing them under his own trademark. Never a great hitter, Irwin was nevertheless an excellent fielder and a crafty baserunner, earning himself the nickname "Foxy." He also had a knack for finding himself in proximity to baseball's miracles. Irwin was a teammate of Charles "Old Hoss" Radbourne during his astonishing 59-win season of 1884. Irwin was also on the field for the first recorded perfect game, driving in the only run in a 1-0 contest. Indeed, he was on the field for *six* perfect games, a fact even more remarkable because when Irwin played gloves weren't standard equipment and pitchers were required to throw underhand. Often games would feature 20 base hits and sometimes as many errors.

After his playing career, Irwin was a professional manager and scout. Upon taking over as manager the University of Pennsylvania's ball team, he claimed he was the first full-time college coach. True or not, he *was* the first president of an American soccer league and he controlled the rights to the first electronic football scoreboard. By 1921, he had been in professional baseball for more than 40 years—from the earliest days of the League to the era of Babe Ruth and the institution of Kenesaw Mountain Landis as the game's first Commissioner.

In July 1921, Irwin boarded a steamer from New York to Boston. When the ship arrived, Irwin wasn't on it. All that remained was a rumpled suit of clothes. His body was never found. In the subsequent investigation into Irwin's disappearance, a curious fact emerged. For over 30 years he had been maintaining two separate households with two different wives, children, and grandchildren, whose existences Irwin had kept secret until his presumed death.

I tell Irwin's story not only because he was instrumental in the invention of the glove—and because his story is too bizarre not to be better known, but also as a reminder as we turn to the next chapter: the baseball glove may seem like a simple object, but we should never hesitate to question what's beneath the surface.

So here's a good Freudian story. Though I cherished my childhood mitt, it was my father's Wilson Catfish Hunter model that really mesmerized me. To my eye, it was huge and adult and I could not wait until I could get a glove that big. I would use it with great surreptitiously in the backyard, always fastidiously returning it to it's proper home in the front closet before anyone would know it was missing. I recall coming across the mitt during a visit to my parent's house a few years back. I was struck that it was nowhere near as large as my memory would have it and I preferred the (now lost) mitt I had at the time.

(VTMSBL player)

Notes

1 United States; SFIA; Sports Marketing Surveys USA; 2007 to 2014.
2 All of the information on Arthur Irwin is contained in his player file at the Giamatti
   Research Center at the National Baseball Hall of Fame and Museum (Irwin, n.d.).
   It is also widely available in contemporary news accounts of the late nineteenth and
   early twentieth century. I am grateful to Cassidy Lent and the staff of the Giamatti
   Research Center for helping me discover this material. The description of Irwin's
   life also figures in my forthcoming article in the Journal of Sport and Social Issues.

1

HISTORIES

We used no mattress on our hands,
No cage upon our face;
We stood right up and caught the ball,
With courage and with grace.

Harry Ellard, *"The Reds of Sixty-Nine"* (1880s)

How can we study the history of a cultural object like the baseball glove?

According to the Spalding sporting goods company, the history of the baseball glove is this:

1877
The First Baseball Glove
[Albert Goodwill] Spalding created the world's first baseball glove, marking the
   transition from bare hands to protective wear. A.G. Spalding's reputation in
   the baseball industry made the once unthinkable "sissy" glove become OK
   to wear ("A Storied History," n.d.)

Would that it were so simple . . .

In John Thorn's *Baseball in the Garden of Eden* (Thorn, 2011), the "official historian of baseball" introduces the reader to one of the fundamental challenges posed to those who are interested in the history of the game: There are a lot of fabrications, mythmaking, selective memories, and sometimes outright lying that go into the story of the "the national pastime." Despite ample evidence that baseball dates back to the eighteenth century and may have been played first—if references in 1798 Jane Austen novels or 1755 Surrey diaries mean anything—in England, early baseball promotors like Spalding and sports writer Henry Chadwick went to great pains to assert America's primacy over the game. "A special commission," Thorn explains,

Spalding's Trade-Marked Catcher's Gloves

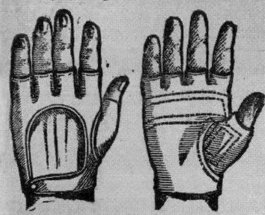

After considerable expense and many experiments we have finally perfected a Catcher's Glove that meets with general favor from professional catchers.

The old style of open backed gloves introduced by us several years ago is still adhered to, but the quality of material and workmanship has been materially improved, until now we can lay claim to having the best line of catcher's gloves on the market. These gloves do not interfere with throwing, can be easily put on and taken off, and no player subject to sore hands should be without a pair of these gloves. We make these gloves in four different grades, as follows:

		Price Per Pair.
No. 0.	SPALDING'S LEAGUE CLUB CATCHER'S GLOVES, made of extra heavy Indian tanned buck, and carefully selected with special reference to the hard service required of them, open back, well padded, and fully warranted......	$2 50
No. 1.	SPALDING'S PROFESSIONAL GLOVES, made of Indian tanned buckskin, open back, well padded, but not quite as heavy material as the No. 0......	2 00
No. 2.	SPALDING'S AMATEUR GLOVES, made of lighter buckskin, open back, well padded and adapted for amateur players......	1 50
No. 3.	SPALDING'S PRACTICE GLOVES, made of light material, open back, well padded......	1 00
No. 4.	SPALDING'S BOY'S GLOVES, open back, well padded and made only in boy's sizes......	1 00

☞ Any of the above Gloves mailed postpaid on receipt of price. In ordering, please give size of ordinary dress gloves usually worn.

A. G. SPALDING & BROS.,

Figure 1.1 **One of the earliest advertisements for "Spalding's Trade-Marked Catcher's Gloves"** **(1884). Smithsonian Institution (from** *Spalding's base ball guide, and official league book for* *1883/1884.* **A.G. Spalding & Bros.)** (*Source*: Retrieved from www.library.si.edu/digital-library/ book/spaldingsbasebal18831chic.)

constituted by sporting-goods magnate . . . Spalding affirmed in 1908, after nearly three years' purported study of the game's true origin, that baseball was assuredly American for it had been created from the fertile brain of twenty-year old Abner Doubleday in Cooperstown, New York, in 1839. Critics of the commission's methods and conclusions soon made an alternative case for the genius of Alexander Cartwright and the Knickerbocker Base Ball Club, founded in New York in 1845.

(Thorn, 2011: xii)

Who invented the game? Pastoral Doubleday or cosmopolitan Cartwright? Whatever the case, Thorn argues, the crucial thing was that the "official story" of baseball was coalescing around the "fact" that baseball was America's game, and that there was something akin to the American character at stake in claiming it. Inconvenient evidence that baseball might have had another origin was ignored.

Of course, by making the case for the rhetorical link between baseball and American national identity, Spalding and Chadwick were in good company. In 1889, Walt Whitman reportedly said of baseball to his friend and chronicler Horace L. Traubel that

it's our game: that's the chief fact in connection with it: America's game: has the snap, go, fling, of the American atmosphere—belongs as much to our institutions, fits into them as significantly, as our constitutions, laws: is just as important in the sum total of our historic life.

(Traubel, 1906: 508)

In that same year, Mark Twain toasted Albert Spalding at a banquet by claiming the game was "the very symbol, the outward and visible expression of the drive, and push, and rush and struggle of the raging, tearing, booming 19th century!" (Brock, 2010).

The notion that baseball is somehow fundamentally analogous to what it means to be American can be traced from Whitman and Twain to Spalding and Chadwick all the way through the twentieth and twenty-first centuries and documentarian Ken Burns' use of baseball as a way to explore "the generational connection of belonging to a vast and complicated American family," or, as the writer Gerald Early puts it in an interview for Burns' *Baseball,* "There are only three things that America will be remembered for 2000 years from now when they study this civilization: The Constitution, Jazz Music, and Baseball" (Burns et al., 1999).

Perhaps because the history of the game is so intimately tied to reflections on what it means and has meant to be American and the cultural practices that define the national character, baseball's history is the subject of ongoing fascination for amateur and professional historians alike. There are a number of organizations for the study of the game's development, and the sport has a wide range of formal and informal venues for the production and sharing of historical research. Among these are the Society for American Baseball Research (SABR), the literary and scholarly journal, *Elysian Fields,* and, of course, the Giamatti Research Center at the National Baseball Hall of Fame and Museum in Cooperstown, New York, which hosts an annual Symposium on Baseball and American Culture. These are just some of the most noteworthy, nationally prominent sites for historical and archival research on the game. Given baseball's popularity, many local libraries, museums, and historical societies also contain a wealth of knowledge about baseball's historical past. Although the store of archival material is finite, it has hardly been completely explored (see Breakout Box 1.1: Practicing Anthropology: Visit an Archive).

That there are so many avenues for the study of baseball history is a testament both to the game's centrality in American life, especially in the nineteenth and early twentieth century, as well as to one of the curious facts about the sport: for a game obsessed with recording quantitative data and statistics, there is an equal and opposite pull to tall-tales and mythmaking. The telling of baseball history is often that of constructing a story that fits an ideal, of picking and choosing the narrative threads that make the most sense. The psychologist Jerome Bruner famously called this tactic "the narrative construction of reality" in which "the act of constructing a narrative,"

> is considerably more than "selecting" events either from real life, from memory, or from fantasy and then placing them in an appropriate order. The events themselves need to be constituted in the light of the overall narrative . . . to be made "functions" of the story.

> (Bruner, 1991: 8)

From this perspective, historical "reality" is as much about a collection of stories as it is about an assortment of facts. Mark Twain was fond of saying "There are three kinds of lies: lies, damned lies, and statistics." He didn't say this about baseball, but as any player can tell you, the stats can be misleading. When a batter hits a bloop single or beats a throw to first on a ball that dribbles off his or her bat, teammates will likely yell, "Looks like a line drive in the books!" as a testament to the way that even the official scorer's record can be the product of selective memory. The historian Hayden White referred to this effort to wrestle competing historical realities into a comprehensible story emplotment. "Most historical sequences can be emplotted in a number of ways," he claimed, "so as to provide different inter-pretations of these events and to endow them with different meanings" (White, 1978: 85). The mode of emplotment—the way that the telling of the story struc-tures events and facts—conditions our understanding of historical reality.

The Spalding/Chadwick origin stories of the game, in which key historical moments are emphasized or de-emphasized, conveniently forgotten, or simply made up in the service of a predetermined narrative, follows this pattern of narrative selectivity. This picking and choosing from the historical record is done in the service of an ideal, that of the game's intimate link to the American character. Thorn explains this type of history thusly:

> It has turned out that Spalding and Chadwick—like the calculating expo-nents of Doubleday and Cartwright—were not mere liars and blowhards. They were conscious architects of legend, shapers of national identity, would-be creators of a useful past and binding archetypes (clever lads, noble warriors, despised knaves, sly jesters, wounded heroes, and so on). In short, they were historians as that term once was understood. They were trying to create a national mythology from baseball, which they identified as America's secular religion because it seemed to supply faith for the faithless and unify them, perhaps in a way that might suit other ends. If in the process of crafting this useful past, certain individuals, events, ball clubs—even competing versions of the game, like those played in New England or Pennsylvania—had to be left along the road in the name of progress, so be it.
>
> (Thorn, 2011: xii–xiv)

That the contradictions at the heart of the story of baseball are at once his-torical and anthropological is made clear in the debt Hayden White explicitly acknowledges to Claude Lévi-Strauss, one of the giants of twentieth-century anthropology. For Lévi-Strauss, the histories of something as culturally signifi-cant to the French like the French Revolution or to Americans like baseball, are necessarily competing mythologies as much as they are chronicles of specific events. Hence, Lévi-Strauss claims:

> authors do not always make use of the same incidents; when they do the incidents are revealed in different lights. And yet these are variations which have to do with the same country, the same period, and the same events—events whose reality is spread across every level of a multilayered structure.
>
> (quoted in White, 1978: 90)

From the standpoint of cultural anthropology, the "history" of baseball is as much about understanding how people have used the stories about the game's origins to explain what they believe about themselves, as it is about finding specific origins of the game's rules, rituals, and traditions. While cultural anthropologists aren't indifferent to questions of origin, they are also invested in what people believe as much as what actually happens at given historical moments. In point of fact, there is no single origin story of the game. Instead, there are collections of events and practices that tend to coalesce at a certain point when we can definitely recognize the game as being played a certain way and representing a certain set values and ideals. To ask who invented baseball, it turns out, is ultimately an unfruitful question. Even if there was one person who "invented" the game—and new archival discoveries may reveal now-forgotten versions of that story—that discovery would be of less interest than the answer to the question of how an idiosyncratic individual expression evolved into a set of cultural practices and beliefs. The how's and why's of the historical narratives are often more significant than the what's and who's.

The same is true of the history of the baseball glove. How and why it became a part of the game and the set of beliefs that evolution sprang from and subsequently engendered is, from the standpoint of cultural anthropology, more interesting than the question of who invented the baseball glove and whether that invention fits into a clear narrative arc. What we discover looking at the glove from these perspectives is that the baseball glove we know today is in many ways very different than the glove that developed in the nineteenth century—and not just from the standpoint of its design and material (the subject of the next chapter), but also in terms of how it serves as a bearer of a whole network of cultural beliefs.

Origins

The novelist L.P. Hartley once wrote, "The past is a foreign country: they do things differently there" (Hartley, 2002: 17). As a motto for a cultural history of the glove, we could do worse. That the glove has a history apart from the history of baseball itself often surprises people. From the standpoint of today's game, the existence of the glove seems as natural and inevitable as the use of a bat and ball. "Flashing the leather" is such a fundamental part of the sport that one of professional baseball's major year-end awards, granted to the best fielders at their respective positions, is a trophy in the shape of a glove: The Rawlings Gold Glove Award, established in 1957. But in terms of the development of the game, it turns out that the glove is a relatively late invention. How late is a matter of no little dispute, but most historians place the introduction of the glove to sometime between the late 1850s and the early 1870s. Throughout much of the nineteenth century, perhaps for nearly 100 years, baseball players fielded the ball barehanded (see Figure 1.2).

Figure 1.2 **Barehanded baseball players (1867). Library of Congress. Left: D. Buchner & Company. (1867). [Ed Andrews, Philadelphia Quakers, baseball card portrait] [Baseball card].** (*Source*: Retrieved from www.loc.gov/pictures/resource/bbc.0035f/.) **Right: D. Buchner & Company. (1867). [John Cahill, Indianapolis Hoosiers, baseball card portrait] [Baseball card].** (*Source*: Retrieved from www.loc.gov/pictures/resource/bbc.0022f/.)

So, who did invent the baseball glove?

Certainly not Albert Goodwill Spalding, although it's easy to see why the sporting goods company that bears his name would want to claim that distinction. But even Spalding, canny self-promoter that he was, didn't claim to have invented the glove himself, instead, in his 1911 memoir he attributed the innovation to a former teammate, Charles Waite, who introduced a glove nearly 40 years before. "I had for a good while felt the need of some sort of hand protection for myself," Spalding explains

> For several years I had pitched in every game played by the Boston team, and had developed severe bruises on the inside of my left hand. Therefore, I asked Waite about his glove. He confessed that he was a bit ashamed to wear it, but had it on to save his hand. He also admitted that he had chosen a color as inconspicuous as possible, because he didn't care to attract attention . . . . Meanwhile, my own hand continued to take its medicine with utmost regularity, occasionally being bored with a warm twister that hurt excruciatingly. Still, it was not until 1877 that I overcame my scruples against joining the "kid-glove aristocracy" by donning a glove.

I found that the glove, thin as it was, helped considerably, and inserted one pad after another until a good deal of relief was afforded. If anyone wore a padded glove before this date, I do not know it.

(Spalding, 1911: 476)

Even though his use of a glove preceded Spalding's by two years, Waite himself was probably a decade late to the game, so to speak. There are a number of competing accounts of the introduction of the glove to baseball, each with their own partisans, but most of these glove historians agree that it was likely a catcher who began the practice rather than a player in the field. The early baseball historian Peter Morris cites an 1886 article in *The Sporting News* attributing the innovation to Albany Knickerbockers catcher Ben De La Vergne who "used gloves when playing behind the bat in the sixties" (Morris, 2010: 289). Furthermore, in an article on the SABR website, Morris expands on that story, writing that:

De La Vergne was one of the brave catchers who played during the antebellum years when baseball first began to earn recognition as the national pastime. Ballplayers of the era wore no protective equipment and, as such, his primary claim to fame is being credited with having been the first ballplayer to defy custom and wear gloves.

However, Morris admits, the evidence is tenuous. "There is no contemporaneous documentation of the claim," he writes, "and, even if there were, there would be no way to prove that De La Vergne's glove had no predecessors." But in the absence of better evidence, Morris decides to go with the Knickerbocker catcher. "Nevertheless, there are no earlier claimants, and thus it seems likely that Ben De La Vergne did indeed pioneer the use of this basic piece of fielding equipment" (Morris, n.d.).

For his part, Noah Liberman, author of *Glove Affairs: The Romance History and Tradition of the Baseball Glove* (Liberman, 2003), points to Doug Allison, catcher for the Cincinnati Red Stockings. In Allison's case, Liberman is able to cite a contemporary account: "*The Cincinnati Commercial* reported on June 28, 1870: 'Allison caught to-day in a pair of buckskin mittens, to protect his hands.' This dry note," Liberman writes, "was tucked into a story on the team's game against the Washington Nationals, and it buried the news, as a reporter would say" (Liberman, 2003: 11).

For Allison, Waite, and De La Vergne, the glove in question was likely no more than a leather palm without fingers designed to offer some modest protection to the catcher, but leaving the fingers free to grip and throw the ball. Some catchers likely wore one on each hand. And it is worth noting that in all

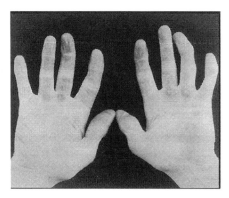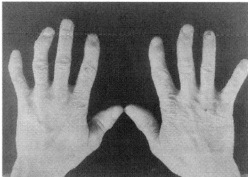

Figure 1.3 **Hands of former professional baseball player, Douglas Allison, showing results of baseball playing. Palmar surface (left); Dorsal surface (right) (February 12, 1889). [NS30, NS31]. OHA78: New Series Photographs.** (*Source*: Otis Historical Archives. National Museum of Health and Medicine.)

of these instances the use of the glove stems from a pragmatic need to protect injured—and in the case of Allison and De La Vergne—horribly mangled hands. One account of De La Vergne has him using a glove to cover a fingertip so broken he'd had to cut it off. After his playing days, Allison had his hands photographed, and the image is a horror show of joints jutting at odd angles, evidence of the punishment he's received in the days of barehanded baseball (see Figure 1.3).

We have somewhat more clarity about the introduction of the padded glove with fingers for players in the field. "To Arthur Irwin, the famous shortstop of the famous Providence team of 1884 belongs the distinction of being the first to introduce the fielder's glove," *The Sporting News* reports in 1915 (see Figure 1.4).

It was in that year that Irwin one day broke the third and fourth fingers of his left hand. In those days the best team only carried ten or twelve men. There was no one to take Irwin's place and so he consulted a glover, bought a buckskin glove many sizes too large for his injured hand, padded it, and sewed the injured fingers together to make way for the bandages. Irwin knew the spectators who knew of his injury would forgive him for appearing on the field with one hand looking much like a boxing glove. He discovered quickly that with the glove, even in his injured condition he could meet the ball solidly, and so even after his broken fingers mended, he continued the use of the glove.

(Irwin player file, National Baseball Hall of Fame)

Irwin's glove caught on, and within a year Irwin, with an entrepreneurial zeal that would characterize much of his life, started marketing them under his own trademark. But even that history is contradicted and complicated by an industrial

Figure 1.4 Arthur Irwin, Philadelphia Quakers [1887]. Digital ID: 56783. Gross & Co. Photographer. (*Source:* The A.G. Spalding Baseball Collection. Repository: The New York Public Library. Photography Collection, Miriam and Ira D. Wallach Division of Art, Prints and Photographs.)

history of the Draper-Maynard Sporting Goods Company who initially manufactured Irwin gloves.

In 1882 the company received a visit from Arthur Irwin, a well-known baseball player who had an idea for a particular sort of baseball glove—padded. Players were then using either their bare hands or a plain glove. Draper & Maynard apparently saw the commercial value of Irwin's idea and made samples that were sent around with their salesmen as an example of custom work that the company could do. The innovative glove, fingerless with a padded palm, created a new market for the company and helped make it

one of the leading sporting goods manufacturers in North America. Somewhat later, another type of glove, with fingers, was made for catchers.

(Freeman et al., 1994: 7–8)

Did Irwin invent the fielder's glove in 1882 or 1884? Was it padded with fingers or was it fingerless? Did Doug Allison or Ben De La Vergne first wear a
catcher's glove? Was Waite's glove flesh-colored to hide it while Spalding's was
darker leather and visible? Did some men fear being called a sissy while others
felt no need to apologize? All of these stories lead us to question what we can
know for certain about the origins and initial adoption of the baseball glove and
why certain stories spring up concerning how people first perceived their use—
these are the questions proper to a history informed by anthropology. At some
point beliefs change, and so with them cultural practices. So much of baseball's
history is shrouded in mystery. What happens in the National Association, the
American Association, and the International Association (the professional
leagues of the nineteenth century where Allison, Waite, and Irwin played), while
perhaps better documented and hence better known, is left to stand in for and
instead of local practices that may correspond with or contradict official history.

What do we know for certain? Not who "invented" the baseball glove, that's
for sure. Instead, let me offer a parallel account to the myth of origin, one
which considers those stories of invention and ingenuity as part of a broader set
of discourses around what is now a game-wide cultural practice but that probably begins as an idiosyncratic local practice. Why the glove appears at all
depends, to some extent, on understanding how the game was changing in the
years during and immediately after the Civil War. What the game looked like in
those years would be recognizable as baseball to fans today even if its name had
not yet contracted into one word and was still being referred to as "Base Ball"
(Morris, 2010). However, in some fundamental respects, the game would be
very different. The setting of the rules by Cartwright in 1845, and the founding
of the first professional league and team—the Cincinnati Red Stockings—in
1846 had made the game less chaotic than it had been in the early part of the
nineteenth century. Before that time players in the field could still get a mem-
ber of the batting team out by "dousing" or "soaking" him with a thrown ball
while the runner was between the bases or by catching a batted ball on one
bounce, and batters could decide whether to run clockwise around the bases
(first to third) or counter-clockwise (third to first). Despite certain codification
taking place in 1840s, the game was still evolving quickly.

In the period during which the glove first made an appearance, pitchers stood
a mere 50 feet from the home plate. The advantage they would seem to gain
from their proximity was offset by the fact that they were only allowed to pitch

underhanded, with the ball released below the hip, and they were prohibited from breaking their wrists. What's more, although batters were given three strikes, they were under no obligation to swing at a ball over the plate if it was not to their liking. Likewise, there was no penalty for errant pitches—unless there was a runner on base who could steal—so there were no walks (Ryczek, 2012). In an effort to speed up the game (a refrain we will hear again) the ruling league of professional baseball, the National Association, instituted the calling of balls and strikes. In the 1870s and 1880s, however, a number of innovations were also tried to give the pitcher more advantage. In addition to letting the pitcher snap his wrist, professional baseball also experimented with allowing the pitcher to make a running delivery, much like in the game of cricket (Ryczek, 2012). By 1893, these modifications and experiments had coalesced to the point that pitching looked fundamentally like what it is today. Baseball had legalized the overhand pitch, legalized the curve ball, and had moved the mound away from the plate to its current distance, 60 ft. 6 in. (Morris, 2010).

In 1877, The *Base Ball News* of Mifflintown, Pennsylvania, included the following news blurb: "A base ball player at Shawton, Wis., a few days ago was struck in the stomach by a thrown ball which knocked him down. He rose quickly, threw the ball to the proper player, then fell again and died in ten minutes" (National Baseball Hall of Fame and Museum. Clippings File "Baseball Gloves"). In all of my research in the history of baseball, this is the only record I have ever seen to a player being killed in this fashion. Players have been struck and killed by balls while at the plate; players have been struck and killed by line drives; but for a player to be killed by a thrown ball while in the field, it can only suggest one thing: he wasn't wearing a glove. If pitching was undergoing a profound transformation in the period between 1860 and 1893, fielding was likewise evolving. The year after this unknown Wisconsin player died on the field Bill McGunnigle, player-manager of the Buffalo Bisons of the International Association professional league, kept a scrapbook of press clippings and notes of the 1878 season. These are collected at the National Baseball Hall of Fame in Cooperstown under the title "Pioneer Baseball."[1] The scrapbook is a unique snapshot of baseball in an era when cities like Binghamton, New York, Manchester, New Hampshire, and London, Ontario had thriving, high-level professional baseball teams. In fact, in 1879, the year after winning the International Association the Buffalo Bisons would join the National League.

From the snippets in McGunnigle's scrapbook, a picture emerges of the day-to-day life of professional ballplayers in the period. Although McGunnigle is sometimes attributed with having invented the catcher's mitt by wearing brick-layers gloves in a game in 1875, it is clear from "Pioneer Baseball" that such an invention hasn't made its way onto the field with any regularity in 1878. Otherwise, we wouldn't have the account of a "Two-Handed Fielder" on the

Auburn, New York team. "He is 'either-handed,' and his name is Roseman," reports a note from the *Auburn Advertiser*. "He plays in the left field and throws to the home plate with either arm. In yesterday's game, he threw out a man at home 'left-handed' and in the previous game he did the same thing with his right" (McGunnigle, 1878: 7). At the same time, during McGunnigle's period, fielding was far more variable than it is today. And "variable" is a euphemism for "awful." More than once in "Pioneer Baseball" McGunnigle feels compelled to record the hapless fielding of the nineteenth-century game. "In a game with the Binghamton Crickets, June 28, the Tecumsehs of London, Ont. Made 20 errors" (McGunnigle, 1878: 61). We also read in a May 6 blurb under the headline "Springfield Errors A-Plenty" that "While Buffalo scored an 11-to-1 win over Springfield, the latter contracted 20 misplays, Cather Curran being responsible for eight. Corcoran, Springfield pitcher, was hard man to hit in '77, but the Buffalos nicked him for nine bingles" (McGunnigle, 1878: 9). For fans of today's game, the stats of the Springfield-Buffalo game are astounding—9 hits ("bingles") against 20 errors. To put this in perspective, take a recent MLB season as a representative sample: In 2016, Major League teams recorded an average of 8.7 hits per game—roughly the same as the Buffalo box score. But the average number of errors per game in 2016 was a mere 0.58 per game. Put another way, it would take the average major-league team more than 34 games to commit as many errors as Springfield or the Tecumsehs did in single games in 1878. In fact, the Major League record for errors in a game by a modern day Major League team (post-1900) is 12 and that last happened in 1903.

In the Harry Ellard poem quoted at the opening of this chapter, which lionizes the courage of Doug Allison's 1869 Reds for not wearing mitts or masks, the consequence of that type of play was some truly ugly games:

> *The game you see them play to-day,*
> *Is tame as it can be;*
> *You never hear of scores like ours—*
> *A hundred and nine to three.*

And the only extent to which the poem indulges in hyperbole is due to the fact that the actual score of the Reds' August 31 victory over the Cincinnati Buckeyes of 103-8 doesn't rhyme with "tame as it can be" (Ellard, 1907: 171).

Far more remarkable than a game with 100 runs or with a greater error total than anyone alive today can remember, in the 1870s having more than one game without errors was considered a miraculous event. After a May 9 game at Lowell, McGunnigle writes;

Aside from the satisfaction of having won a game from a strong team, it is with considerable pride that we point to the fact that our men played without an error. This is so unusual that old ball-men can sit down and tell every game they played in, when such a record was made. . . It discloses the justly remarkable fact that the other members of our nine have played three games this week without making a single error. We believe this is a record made by no other team either in the International or the [National] League so far this season.

(McGunnigle, 1878: 9)

Hence, one of the last clippings McGunnigle includes in "Pioneer Baseball" is an editorial in the *Cleveland Leader* on the relative virtue of fielding and how it has helped McGunnigle's team:

A careful glance through the records of both the League and International players for the season just closed brings to light some curious facts. For instance, take the Bostons. In fielding they rank first, but in batting they are far down the list. Yet they come out the champions. In the International Association the Buffalos rank comparatively poor as batters, but in fielding they stand first. These facts go to show, notwithstanding the general opinion to the contrary that games are won by the clear, cool, careful headwork of the players on the field, not by their tremendous batting. Good batting is a fine requisite to good playing, but scientific fielding, according to the facts, is what takes the pennant.

(McGunnigle, 1878: 243)

In an era with scores of runs (predominately on singles), 20 errors in the field were common, and three errorless games in a row was unheard of, imagine the competitive advantage a player would have if the practice of "scientific fielding" were extended to the equipment used in the game. Catching a batted baseball barehanded is difficult and dangerous. Baseballs—which can be thrown and hit at speeds of upwards of 100 mph—hurt. A piece of equipment that could both protect the hand and facilitate more efficient fielding would undoubtedly privilege the teams and players who chose to utilize it.

This competitive advantage is on conspicuous display in another celebratory team poem, this one composed for an 1860 Christmas ball held by the Mercantile Baseball Club of Philadelphia. In a poem in the Hall of Fame titled, "Owe'd 2 Base Ball in Three Cant-oh's!" we learn of the squad's heroic first basemen:

Then "Bispham" comes next, you'd expect from his looks,
He was given to study, addicted to books,
And you'd little suspect there was much in the man,

Till you saw him at play—then beat him who can.
His favorite position is on the first base,
And he stands like a statue, always right about face,
With his hands in a pair of thick gloves all encased,
Which never miss holding the ball once embraced.
And I pity the 'batter' who when the ball's fair,
If its short, tries to make the 'first base' when he's there.
The 'batter' itself may be good enough—though
He's sure to be put out, and his cake is all 'dough.'

(National Baseball Hall of Fame and Museum, 1860;
Italics – my emphasis)

Thinking about this poem in light of the counter-narrative I am trying to tell, it is significant that, written in 1860, "Owe'd 2 Base Ball" is the earliest contemporaneous reference to gloves being used in play that we know—predating the stories of Allison and De La Vergne's "inventions" by a number of years. But the element of the poem even more worth noting is how un-noteworthy the glove is. I emphasize it; the writer of the poem doesn't. The idea of his first baseman wearing thick gloves doesn't merit much pause except as a way to explain how the bookish "Bispham" becomes manlier when donning them.

This last part is extremely important however, because given how early "Owe'd 2 Base Ball" is, Bispham's heroic transformation contradicts the most widely accepted belief about the early adoption of the baseball glove: that players who used them were met with ridicule for their perceived lack of masculinity.

So strong is the version of the glove's myth in which early users are called sissies and unmanly that we can trace it from Spalding's 1911 memory that Charles Waite was ashamed to play with a glove (and hence wore a flesh-colored model) throughout the twentieth century to today when the Spalding company refers to the "unthinkable 'sissy' glove." But this belief in the perceived unmanliness of the glove is hardly exclusive to Spalding and the company that bears his name. In fact, throughout the literature on the glove, both by reputable historians and by popular writers, the association between the glove and beliefs about masculinity persist. Consider the range of writers who promote this idea:

Old players—Former Yankee, Frankie Frisch, 1962: We had to make stops with our bare hands. Now they have snaring nets they call baseball gloves. The first baseman's glove is like a basketball hoop with a net in it . . . . Baseball players today do not have the same urge, the old fighting spirit that characterized the ballplayers of what I call the old-timer's era.

(Morris, 2010: 293)

Sportswriters (*Sports Illustrated* May 7, 1990)—In 1875 a St. Louis outfielder and first baseman named Charles C. Waite began wearing flesh-colored gloves with the fingers cut out of the right glove to allow him to throw. They were flesh-colored because Waite did not want to draw attention to himself. Fans and opponents called him a sissy, anyway.

(Wulf, 1990)

Old players and sportswriters (Gutman and McCarver, 1996)—Waite chose a tan work glove with an opening in the back, hoping fans and opposing players wouldn't notice. It didn't work. He was ridiculed unmercifully as a sissy.

(Gutman and McCarver, 1996: 24)

The "nation's attic" (*Smithsonian*, 2013)—These were the days when the measure of a man was the number of calluses on his fingers and of broken bones in his hand. Wearing a glove just wasn't manly.

(Stamp, 2013)

Historians (Liberman, 2003)—[Allison] was razzed by opposing players and fans. No mention is found of any other player wearing a glove for another five years.

(Liberman, 2003: 11)

Children's authors (Campbell, 2002)—Until the late 1800s, baseball players did not wear baseball gloves, because it was thought "unmanly."

(Campbell, 2002: 21)

Even Canadian childhood literacy experts promote this belief as part of their reading curriculum. The author of a 4th grade reader uses Arthur Irwin as an example of Canadian national pride—and common sense:

Today we have all kinds of protective sports equipment to wear. This helps to keep players safe and prevents many injuries. Imagine playing a sport without all that protective gear. A Toronto ballplayer named Arthur Irwin decided to do something about some of those injuries. One day, in 1884, he showed up at a game with a makeshift padded glove. His teammates kidded him and called him a sissy. After the game, they learned that Arthur was able to play the whole game with two broken fingers! Before long, everyone was copying his great idea of wearing a padded glove.

(Summers, 2011: 81)

This last example, *Raising a Reader: Improving Reading and Writing Skills (Grade 4)* was written in 2011, that is to say, 100 years after Spalding's memoir first hinted that Waite found wearing a glove shameful. For a century, ballplayers and baseball fans have believed that the players who introduced the baseball glove were taunted as sissies. While it is likely true that some players were teased on those grounds— baseball players are notorious for ribbing their teammates[2]—the historical record doesn't turn up much in the way of contemporary confirmation of that belief. In fact, "Owe'd 2 Base Ball" and McGunnigle's "Pioneer Baseball" suggest a pre-vailing counter-narrative: that the glove provide a competitive advantage while at the same time protecting players from injury. It is these characteristics, as much as beliefs about manliness and unmanliness in the game, that color the contem-porary debates about adopting the glove. Hence in 1867, *The Detroit Free Press* reports:

We have noticed in all the matches played thus far that the use of gloves by the players was to some degree a customary practice, which we think, can-not be too highly condemned, and are of the opinion that the [Ionia] Custers would have shown a better score if there had been less buckskin on their hands.

(Morris, 2010: 289)

At least at this early moment in the glove's evolution, success on the diamond rather than beliefs about masculinity predominate.

We can see that what's at stake in the competing origin stories of the glove are questions about two different modes of performance—the performance of gender and performance on the field. Although the introduction of the glove makes an undeniable impact on the game in terms of improved fielding and fewer injuries, the story that tends to predominate is the one having to do with how the glove is perceived to emasculate the wearer. In an influential essay by Judith Butler, she argues that gender, as it is expressed in a given cultural and historical moment, is always a materially enacted performance that conveys meaning. The conditions of possibility for those meanings "are necessarily con-strained by available historical conventions. The body is not a self-identical or merely factic materiality; it is a materiality that bears meaning" (Butler, 1988: 521). From the standpoint of the history of the baseball glove and the habitus it embodies, because baseball is so deeply tied to what it means to be an American, in a very real sense, the history of the baseball glove is illustrative of the history of American masculinity—particularly as it is articulated in the latter half of the nineteenth century. "Honest men, good Americans," claimed Teddy Roosevelt in an 1886 speech, have "need of the rougher, manlier virtues, and above all the virtue of personal courage, physical as well as moral." These men should be:

> capable of devoted adherence to a lofty ideal; but in addition we must be vigorous in mind and body, able to hold our own in rough conflict with our fellows, able to suffer punishment without flinching, and, at need, to repay it in kind with full interest.

(Roosevelt, 1886: 555)

For Roosevelt, part of what it meant to be an American man meant to be physically strong, courageous, and able to dish out and receive violence. This was the nexus of "The Manly Virtues and Practical Politics," as the speech was called, and this ideal, made explicit in Roosevelt's rhetoric is implicit in the popular portrayal of American masculinity from the cowboys populating the western to the hardboiled heroes of Raymond Chandler novels and ultimately to the action heroes of today. It is easy to see why wearing a baseball glove, thereby suggesting that a player was less physically courageous or "flinching" in the face of punishment, was deemed unmanly in the midst of the overwhelming discourse about what it meant to be a man in the nineteenth and twentieth centuries.

At the same time, for many players in the nineteenth century, a competing and equally compelling discourse coalesces around a set of other characteristics associated with the American character, namely ingenuity, entrepreneurship, and the pursuit of competitive advantage (Akcigit et al., 2017; Ferguson, 1962; Lasch, 1991). Hence if we are to assume that there is at least something to the tales of players being called "sissies" and the like for wearing gloves, figures like Spalding and Irwin are able to combat that discourse by transforming their concession to physical safety into success on the field and financial gain.

In terms of the history of material objects, cultural anthropologists often make sense of competing discourses by turning their attention to patterns of adoption by which material goods enter into common practice. "In seeking explanations for the trajectories of artefacts manufactured in the factories of capitalist, industrial societies," the influential behavioral archaeologist Michael Brian Schiffer explains: "behaviouralists have found it useful to think of product types as having life histories. The life history of a product type, such as portable radio or electric car, consists of three processes: invention, commercialization, and adoption" (Schiffer, 2000: 81).

At some point, local practices involving material objects evolve into common practices. Baseball players wearing makeshift gloves stuffed with padding, grass, leaves, and sometimes even meat (Light, 2005: 380) transform their ideas into codified patents and begin to sell their ideas. What begins as idiosyncratic innovation transforms itself into standard operating procedure.

In his influential book *Subculture: The Meaning of Style*, Dick Hebdige discusses this process as one in which the meanings of cultural practices transform from one of deviance to one of embrace. "In highly complex societies like ours," he writes, "which function through a finely graded system of divided (i.e. specialized) labor," Certain groups have, at any given moment "more say, more opportunity to make the rules, to organize meaning, while others are less favourably placed, have less power to produce and impose their definitions of the world on the world" (Hebdige, 1979: 14). Hebdige examined the way that punk sensibility, at first alien to and alienated from dominant British society—"forever condemned to act out alienation"—could coalesce as a style marking out class, race, and gender positions, and which, because of its distinctiveness begins "to strike its own eminently marketable pose" (Hebdige, 1979: 93). The codes of punk ultimately get adopted by the mainstream, repackaged and marketed. Hebdige calls this hegemonic process one of recuperation, which takes, he claims, "takes two characteristic forms:"

(1) the conversion of subcultural signs (dress, music, etc.) into mass-produced objects (i.e. the commodity form);
(2) the 'labelling' and re-definition of deviant behavior by dominant groups – the police, the media, the judiciary (i.e. the ideological form) (Hebdige, 1979: 94).

Of course, the price one pays for recuperation—adoption by the dominant group—is losing one's outsider status, you can't be "punk" and mainstream at the same time.

We can understand the adoption and evolution of the glove in this light. While initially a practice associated with deviance from the norm—maybe of gender, maybe of fair play, possibly of both, maybe of neither—after all, it is somewhat unclear how to parse the *Detroit Free Press* reporter's claim that the use of the glove "cannot be too highly condemned"—ultimately, gloves are embraced as part of the official status quo and become both marketable commodities and part of the fabric of the game as enshrined in the rules. These two processes operate simultaneously throughout the 1880s and 1890s. In his book, *Glove Affairs*, Noah Liberman takes the position that historians miss something about the rich pre-history of baseball by emphasizing the modern game associated with Cartwright's rules:

Baseball's bible, *Total Baseball*, begins its "Famous Firsts" section with Cartwright's rule book in 1845, ignoring the more vital firsts (such as balls, strikes, and bases) that came well before and implying that a clerical event marked the beginning of the game we now play. That's an arbitrary way to make sense of a long evolution.

(Liberman, 2003: 12)

While I am sympathetic to Liberman's position with respect to the obscured historical origin of the glove, I think that the moment at which a practice of the game gets codified in the rules is extremely significant because it represents the point at which competing discourses and local customs transform into sanctioned practice. In the case of the baseball glove the recuperation Hebdige identifies take place in a number of "official" discourses.

First, the glove is sanctioned as a recognizable object in the records of the patent office.

In the 1885 patent for a baseball glove by George H. Rawlings, the rationale for granting a patent hews pretty clearly to one of our common narratives: protection of the hands (see Figure 1.5). "The glove is intended especially for the use of base-ball players and cricketers, the pads being for the prevention of the bruising of the hands when catching the ball." What's noteworthy about Rawlings' application is that Rawlings claims that the design and purpose of the glove aren't what constitute its innovation "I do not claim any novelty in the general shape of the glove, nor in the material of which its outerpart is formed. It is not broadly new to pad the glove upon the inner side for the purpose stated, and this I do not claim" (Rawlings, 1885). Instead, what constitutes the glove's novelty is the rubber padding which provides flexibility. It's clear from Rawlings' justification that the glove is already a fairly common piece of equipment as of 1885.

The second place one sees the recuperation of the glove is across the pages of the various yearly guides to baseball published in the latter half of the nineteenth century. These compendia—often running to hundreds of pages—include summaries of the previous season, notable events, including a "Necrology" section of player's deaths, player stats, rules, commentary on the rules, and finally, since many of these guides were published by sporting goods manufacturers, at the end of every guide are pages of advertisements for sports equipment.

By far the most successful and longest running of these guides were *Spalding's Official Base Ball Guides*, which began publication in 1877, and the *Reach's Base Ball Guide*, published by the Alfred J. Reach sporting goods company of Philadelphia, which started in 1883 (see Figures 1.6 and 1.7). The two guides published separately until they merged in 1940, an arrangement that only lasted two years until *The Sporting News* took over as the *Official Baseball Record*. In announcing the merger,

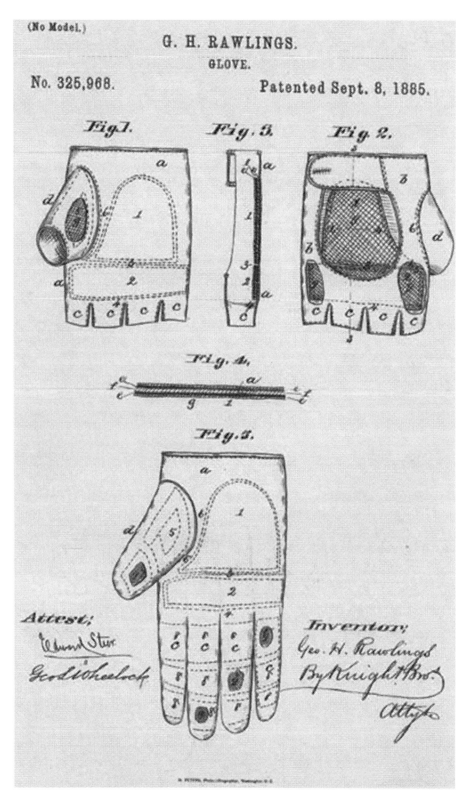

Figure 1.5 **George H. Rawlings, "Glove," (1885). Patent # 325,968.** (*Source*: Google Patents, 1885.)

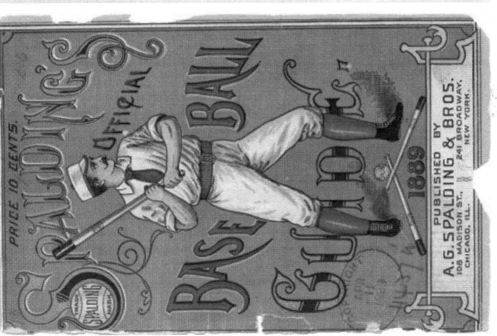

Figures 1.6 and 1.7 Spalding's Base Ball Guide (1889). [Library of Congress] Reach's Base Ball Guide (1884). (Source: www.19cbaseball. com/images/reachs-official-american-association-baseball-guide-1884.jpg.)

however, the editors noticed that "The coalition of the two guides marks another step in the literature of the national game and every effort will be made by the publishers to continue the combined guide as the outstanding authoritative chronicle of base ball" (LinWeber, n.d.).

The editors of the 1942 guide strike a relatively modest tone when compared to the nineteenth-century guides. The full title of the 1895 Spalding guide is:

> *Spalding's Base Ball Guide and Official League Book for 1895, Edited by Henry Chadwick: A Complete Hand Book Of The National Game Of Base Ball, Containing The Full Official League Records For 1894, Together With The New Code Of Playing Rules As Revised By The Committee Of Rules. Attached To Which Are Explanatory Notes, Giving A Correct Interpretation Of The New Rules. A Prominent Feature Of The Guide For 1895 Is The New Championship Record; Added To Which Are The Complete Pitching Records Of 1894 And Special Chapters On The Fielding And Base Running Of 1894, Together With Interesting Records Of The Most Noteworthy Contests, Incidents And Occurrences Of The Eventful Season Of 1894, Occurring In The College Arenas As Well As In That Of The Professional Clubs.*

(Spalding Guide, 1895)

Hyperbolic titles aside, the editors weren't necessarily overselling their case. If Hebdige argues that fashions and practices move from subculture to dominant culture both commercially and ideologically, it is in the guides that we can most directly see the evolution of the glove in both its commodity and its ideological form. The 1895 Spalding Guide provides an excellent snapshot of the point at which the "deviance" of the baseball glove sees its recuperation into the official discourse of the game as the editors assess its impact on the development of pitching, fielding, and batting and the glove's role in those changes.

Hence—the evolution of pitching is symbiotically linked to the introduction and development of the glove. As the rules for pitching changed and pitchers got faster, the glove represented salvation to the man behind the plate.

> The experience of the past season in connection with the limit of speed in pitching presents some valuable suggestions which team managers will do well to bear in mind this year. Some years ago, the swift pitching—which had then about reached the highest point of speed—proved to be so costly in its wear and fear upon the catchers that clubs had to engage a corps of reserve catchers, in order to go through a season's campaign with any degree of success. Afterward, however, the introduction of the protective

"mitts" led to some relief being afforded the catchers who had been called upon to face the swift pitching of the "cyclone" pitchers of the period.

(Spalding Guide, 1895: 71)

At the same time that gloves are making it possible for pitchers to throw faster and use a greater variety of pitches (without depleting a stockpile of catchers), they are also threatening run productivity "The totals of 814 single figure games against 741 double figure contests shows that the pitching is not yet overpowered by the batting, though the use of the big mitts in infield work had much to do with the scoring of single figure games" (Spalding Guide, 1895: 94). All of this leads, in the 1895 Spalding Guide to a fundamental question—can one compare the fielding expertise of a player in the pre-glove era to a player using a glove in the field after their introduction?

Some splendid fielding was done in 1894, but as a whole it was not superior to that of 1893, or even to that of 1892. One reason for this was the introduction of the catcher's "big mitt" in the infield work—something that should not have been allowed. It was due to this fact that the batting scores were not larger the past season than they were in 1893, the big mitt on the hands of infielders enabling them to stop hard hit "bounders" and "daisy cutters" which, but for the use of the mitts, would have been clean earned base hits. This gave the infielders an opportunity to materially lessen the base hit record.

(Spalding Guide, 1895: 117)

For fans of the game, one will likely hear echoes of perennial debates: Which is the "better" game: that which promotes defense (pitching and fielding), or that which celebrates offense (hits and runs scored)? Which records are more significant: those of a bygone era when the game was harder, the season shorter, the mound lower, etc. or contemporary records achieved under current rules. All of this comes to a head in the 1895 Spalding Guide around the issue of whether or not infielders should be able to wear a glove—any glove—in the field. The editors spend no small amount of editorial ink adjudicating this:

In regard to the wearing of the catcher's "big mitt" by infielders in 1894, it is worthy of note that that first-class utility man of them Philadelphia team, "Lave" Cross, while wearing a catcher's mitt as third baseman—a large one at that, too—used it to such advantage that it was next to impossible for a ball hit to his position to get by him. At times it was simply laughable to see him stop ground hits. To wear such gloves is making a travesty of skillful infield work in stopping hard hit, bounding or ground balls. But with the speedy batting of the hard ball now in use, the stopping of hard hit balls in the infield becomes dangerous to the fingers without the aid of small gloves. But no such glove as the catcher's mitt should be allowed to be used save by the catchers or first basemen. In this position the "mitt" in question is a necessity in view of the great speed of the pitcher's delivery and the extremely wild, swift throwing from the field positions to first base. It should be borne in mind that in the days when gloves were not worn, when the pitching was far less swift than now, even then broken and split fingers marked nearly every contest, and behind the bat four catchers were needed where one or two will now suffice.

(Spalding Guide, 1895: 121)

In 35 years, we have come a long way from "Bispham" the Philadelphia first basemen in 1860 ("With his hands in a pair of thick gloves all encased/ Which never miss holding the ball once embraced") to Lave Cross "making a travesty of skillful infield work" by virtue of wearing a glove. But to read the 1895 Spalding Guide from an anthropological perspective, it is clear that in this 35-year period, we are well within the terrain laid out by Lévi-Strauss (and Hayden White) where "variations which have to do with the same country, the same period, and the same events" are being negotiated, debated, and analyzed to identify an appropriate response to a phenomenon. Given that the use of the glove has become at once so ubiquitous and so idiosyncratic, it therefore comes as no surprise that the 1895 Spalding Guide also marks the first appearance of the glove in the official rules of the game:

RULE 19. SECTION 1. SECTION. 2. The catcher and first baseman are permitted to wear a glove or mitt of any size, shape or weight. All other players are restricted to the use of a glove or mitt weighing not over ten ounces, and measuring in in circumference around the palm of the hand not over fourteen inches.

(Spalding Guide, 1895: 142)

In Hebdige's terms, this is the moment at which an "aberrant" or at least ungoverned practice undergoes the "labelling and re-definition" which identifies use of a glove as a dominant practice. For anthropologists who study sports, the introduction of rules is what allows sporting contests to move from localized community practices to broader, even global activities. Standardized rules mean a standardized practice whose proper activities need to be communicated

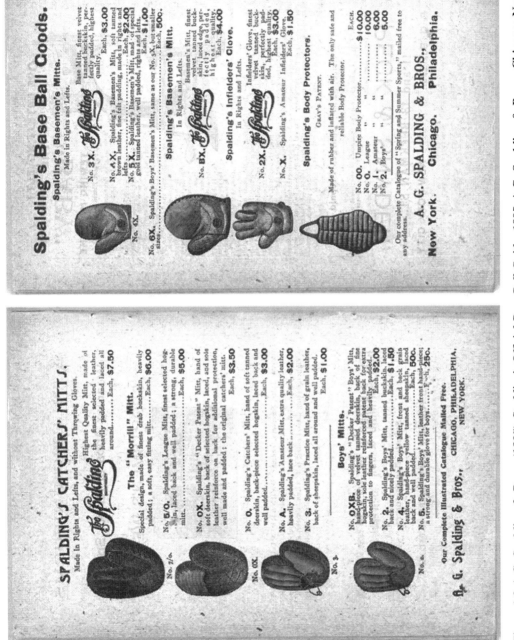

Figure 1.8 A.G. Spalding & Bros. (1895) *Spalding's Official Base Ball Guide, 1895.* A.G. Spalding & Bros., Chicago; New York. [Periodical] (pp. 196, 198). (*Source:* Retrieved from the Library of Congress, www.loc.gov/item/spalding.00148/.)

across wider communities (Besnier et al., 2017). Moreover—and not at all surprisingly—it is clear that as part of the ideological recuperation of the glove, there is a corresponding effort to convert this heretofore idiosyncratic practice into a marketable commodity, an equally important element in Hebdige's framework (see Figure 1.8). The more rules in sports, the more commitment to bureaucratic procedure (Blanchard, 1995), but also the more commitment to equipment. Hence, in the years immediately preceding the publication of the 1895 Spalding Guide, the Spalding company has also been marketing an increasingly specialized array of gloves and mitts for catchers, first basemen, and infielders. At the moment of adoption, Spalding has created a ready-made supply of objects to fill the ideological demand.

Signposts

The glove's emergence as a consumer good is, naturally, a key part of understanding the range of meanings that accrue to it. Ultimately, we will address its function as a commodity to come to grips with the "value" a glove holds as an object of both economic and anthropological interest. Of course, the history of the glove's development—as a piece of equipment, as a bearer of meaning, or as a consumer good—doesn't end with its 1895 codification in the rules or with the proliferation of produced and advertised models in the back pages of the Reach and Spalding guides. In fact, as we'll see in the next chapter, the changes in the rules of baseball are a good place to see the material evolution of the glove and the set of beliefs and practices that accrue around it. The material history of the glove is, of course, part of its history. For now, however, before considering its material evolution more closely, rather than continue in a straightforward chronology from 1895 to the present, I would like to set a few signpost episodes in the historical development that point the way to a more sustained consideration of an analysis of material and meaning that we'll rejoin in subsequent chapters.

Gloves on the Field

Perhaps one of the most idiosyncratic rituals of the game surrounding the glove—and one that was ultimately enshrined in the rules when it was banned—was the habit of players, particularly outfielders, leaving their gloves in the field while their team was at bat. This quaint picture of baseball history where players blithely left their equipment behind tended to be painted in egalitarian terms with players, like apostles in the early church, simply abandoning their possessions to be picked up by other players. The reality behind this practice tended to be far more prosaic. Today's dugouts—especially professional ones—are spacious, even luxurious spaces with individual storage for players' personal gear: helmets, bats, and gloves, not to mention the containers for water, energy drinks, sunflower seeds, and bubble gum.

Breakout Box 1.1: Practicing Anthropology: Visit an Archive

One of the first questions a cultural anthropologist, an intellectual historian, or a cultural theorist is likely to ask is "how did we get to now?" In the case of complex cultural practices, the answers to that question are often so complicated and so contradictory as to produce whole books and even whole fields of study dedicated to answering that question (How has the practice of Catholicism changed over the centuries? How do the Roma people define themselves?). In the case of a material object of anthropological interest like the baseball glove, the answer might at first blush seem more straightforward, after all, we're dealing with only a small piece of a larger cultural practice. But when one takes into account how local customs and practices deviate from more universal standards, the material goods associated with those practices reveal themselves to be just as complicated as the phenomena from which they derive.

Archival research is the cornerstone of the work of the historian, but it is also extremely important for anthropologists interested in how material culture is embodied at a local level or in official discourses. In Kaori O'Connor's book *Lycra*, which took her into the archives of the Dupont company and family, she writes that this was not always the case:

Archival records—like statistical data and collective representations— were formerly regarded as antithetical to ethnography and to the material gained through direct observation. Archival research was not considered "real" anthropology. Fortunately, archives are now becoming accepted as valid ethnographic sites, with the anthropologist of the field and the present also acting as the anthropologist of the past.

(O'Connor, 2011: 21)

One of the places to see that local historical development is close at hand in your public or university library, historical society, or museum dedicated to regional history. Given baseball's historical significance throughout the country—and throughout much of the world, and the fact that most colleges and universities field baseball teams, university special collections and state and regional archives are often treasure troves of baseball-related materials.

Assignment: Take the opportunity to visit one of these institutions to see how baseball was played and how gloves were—or maybe weren't—used in your town in days past. What did the gloves look like? Were they used by all of the players? How does the game of baseball look the same as—or different from—the way it does today?

Does your collection contain objects? Is it possible to examine them? If actual pieces of equipment aren't available, what images/descriptions of baseball gloves and players are there? How do these images change over time? How are gloves advertised and sold in local newspapers? What is the rhetoric of these materials? If your institution collects and catalogs ephemera, items that were meant to be seen or used for a short period of time and then discarded, ask if the collection has any items related to baseball. Advertisements, fliers, and posters can be as useful to the historically minded cultural anthropologist as newspaper articles, letters, memoirs, and photographs. Taken together, these items help give a sense of how people actually engaged in cultural practices using objects like the glove and the constellation of beliefs and aspirations surrounding them.

Before you go, contact the librarian, archivist, or collections specialist to set up an appointment. Tell them what types of material you're looking for. Often professionals with expertise in historical materials will know of idiosyncratic material in their collections that doesn't comfortably fit under your search topic but which nevertheless fills in the historical picture you're trying to describe. Ask before you go if the collection you are visiting allows researchers to take their own photographs of items and documents or if there is a fee to reproduce documents and images of objects. Whatever the case, bring paper and a pencil (most historical collections won't allow pens) and be prepared to take detailed notes including record numbers of the items you study.

Finally, be open to the possibility that something you're not looking for could be every bit as exciting and informative as the ostensible purpose of your archive visit. For example, Middlebury College professor Karl Lindholm tells the story of visiting the Henry Sheldon Museum (a local history museum where I also did some of the research for this book) and discovering that the Cuban Giants, one of the most famous teams of black players in the nineteenth century, had traveled to tiny Middlebury, Vermont to play a series of games.

"The Cuban Giants," Lindholm writes,

This seminal black team, barnstormed all the way to Vermont? To Middlebury! Played the College boys?... This information, along with its source, these magnificent artifacts, the broadsides, constituted for me the most profound "A-Ha!" moment I have had doing baseball research. All writers and researchers await eagerly these "A-Ha!" moments—and they come all too rarely.

(Lindholm, 2016)

Figure 1.9 **Lee Tannehill (1904). Murnane, T. H. (Timothy Hayes), 1852–1917.** *How to Play Base Ball.* (*Source*: T.H. Murnane. New York, American Sports Publishing Co., 1904.)

When you go to your collection, be ready for your "A-Ha" moment. You never know when they'll happen. In the research for this book, one of many "A-Ha" moments for me came when looking at a series of manuals on how to play baseball I found at the Giamatti Research Center in Cooperstown, New York (see Figure 1.9). This photo, from the 1904 edition of *How to Play Base Ball*, depicts Lee Tannehill of the Chicago Americans demonstrating "how to catch a ball which is over the head. This sort of catch is the most sensational a player can make." What makes the catch even more exciting, as sharp-eyed readers will note, is that Tannehill is catching the ball with his bare right hand despite wearing a glove on the left. Was this a common practice? Did players, even once the glove was clearly established, still try to snag line drives barehanded? Was this possibly a prank photo? The last time players were recorded as playing barehanded was 1901 or 1902, but could this photo be evidence of a transition from a bygone practice to a new standard? The same photo does not appear in the 1903 edition of *How to Play Base Ball*, nor does it do so in the 1905 edition or any subsequent ones. I asked baseball historian Tom Simon about this image, and he said that the photograph was almost definitely staged since it is unlikely that the cameras available at the time would be able to catch a ball in mid-air in the instant before it was caught. But he could shed no light on the idiosyncrasy of the barehanded catch. "It certainly would be 'the most sensational a player can make,'" he laughed, but as to why this photo would be in a how-to manual, he couldn't say. Although there are many photographic images from the late nineteenth and early twentieth century that demonstrate players catching the ball barehanded, I have never seen an image like the one of Tannehill in Murnane's guide. And so, this is both my "A-Ha!" moment, and my "Hmm" moment at the same time as it provokes the need for more archival digging. . .

Suggested Reading

Simon, Tom, ed. *Deadball Stars of the National League.* Washington, DC: Brassey's, Inc., 2004.

Early dugouts were much more crowded and less well-appointed, with barely enough room for players, let alone a tumble of gear. Bats might have been stood up in a box or a bin. Players didn't wear batting helmets before 1956. Batting gloves weren't introduced until 1964. Beyond catcher's equipment, which is specialized and easily identifiable, the only other portable, removable object is the player's glove. Rather than add to the clutter of the dugout and risk losing them in the jumble of teammates' similar looking gloves (colored gloves weren't available until the early 1970s), players would simply leave them in the field rather than slow down the transition from offense to defense between half-innings.

Although the practice developed for practical reasons, predictably, there were hazards. Players would trip over gloves while tracking fly balls, and grounders could career off gloves and change course, sending presumably foul balls into fair play. Furthermore, a glove left in the field was also the target for another longstanding tradition of the game: the practical joke. In *The Cultural Encyclopedia of Baseball,* Jonathan Fraser Light describes players "stuffing them with rocks, dirt, mice, frogs, lizards, and snakes. Eddie Stanky, tabbed as one of the worst offenders, once hid Bill Rigney's glove under second base." Thinking of baseball as a cultural practice, one noteworthy aspect of these pranks is how often they were aimed at one of the defining characteristics baseball players—their generally superstitious nature, and their belief in bad luck. "A dead rat was put into Yankee Phil Rizzuto's glove," Light continues, "as he was deathly afraid of rodents. Johnny Pesky, a Hearts card player, found the deadly queen of spades in his glove" (Light, 2005: 382). A practice so ripe for pranking, mishap, and altering the course of the game was perhaps inevitably destined to change. In November of 1953, Major League Baseball Commissioner Ford Frick and the Playing Rules Committee met and changed the rule regarding equipment left on the field. The new rule (3.16) read: "Members of the offensive team shall carry all gloves and other equipment off the field and to the dugout while their team is at bat. No equipment shall be left lying on the field, either in fair or foul territory" (Poliquin, 2013).

In Peter Morris' *A Game of Inches*, he relays that

the impetus for banning the practice may have been provided by a game between the [Chicago] White Sox and [Washington] Senators on July 12, 1952. The hometown Senators were behind 1-0 in the fifth when Chicago shortstop Sam Dente tripped over the glove of opposing number Pete Runnells on what would have been the third out. Washington then rallied for two runs and hung on for a 2-1 victory.

(Morris, 2010: 430)

But here as with the introduction of the glove itself, even if the rule made sense from a safety and competitive standpoint, baseball traditionalists resisted the cultural change. *The Sporting News* reported that the American League refused to follow the rule threatening to "make our own interpretation" (Daniel, 1954). Well-known sports columnist, Shirley Povich offered the opinion that

what the rules committee may have come up with in addition to an unpopular regulation is a hot potato. The new rule is practically an invitation for stalling when a team is trying to delay a game for rain or other purposes. The rules people have saddled the umpires with new troubles in enforcing the regulations.

(Povich, 1954)

As many anthropologists and other observers (Berry, 2008; Fadiman, 2012) who have looked at what happens to longstanding rituals expressions of beliefs when confronted with disruptive new conditions—new homes, new medical practices, new foods, new rules and laws—cultural practices don't just change overnight—not even over the off season. Acculturation to new conditions is a process not an on-off switch, and each society and its individual members are better or less well suited to cultural change. "A society's ecological context provides conditions for the development of collective cultural practices," the social psychologist John Berry writes (Berry, 2008: 25), and the ecological context of baseball is often mired in hidebound tradition and adherence to outmoded practices for the sake of that tradition (Gmelch, 1992, 2001; Lewis, 2004). Baseball's lifers often magnify that recalcitrance. "The phenomenon of cultural lag may also be accompanied by the individual-level phenomenon of behavioral lag" (Berry, 2008: 31).

Hence, some of the well-known characters of the game had the most trouble adapting to the new rule. Yankees manager Casey Stengel complained:

> There is no sensible reason for the rule which forces the players to carry their gloves off the field after each half inning . . . We are trying every which way to speed up games, Now we have a rule which makes for delays. I don't get it.

(Morris, 2010: 430)

For his part, Chicago White Sox manager Paul Richards argued that "you're going to have three-hour games, and a lot of tired players if they have to put up with that nonsense. The games are too long now. They were supposed to be looking for ways to speed 'em up, and they slow 'em up" (quoted in Povich, 1954). Here, as in many cases throughout the history of the game, two or more competing sets of beliefs govern the willingness to adopt a practice. Hank Greenberg took an aesthetic stance to the issue, claiming that all of the gloves in the field looked "sloppy." And perhaps reflecting on the way that many momentous cultural changes seem less disruptive from the vantage point of hindsight longtime manager Ralph Houk, admitted that:

> I know when the rule was changed, nobody could believe it would work . . . But now I think it would really look funny if you saw all those gloves lying around on the field. Actually, it's amazing to me that they didn't change the rule for a long time before they did.

(Poliquin, 2013)

How Big is Too Big?

In April 1972, Henry J. Peters, president of minor league baseball, sent a memo to all of the clubs he represented, notifying them of the changes adopted by the Official Playing Rules Committee in March of that year. Of special note was

Rule 1.14, which he saw fit to attach in its entirety along with a diagram. Rule 1.14 read, in part:

> Each fielder, other than the first baseman or catcher, may use or wear a leather glove. The measurements covering the size of glove shall be made by measuring front side or ball receiving side of glove. The tool or measuring tape shall be placed to contact the surface or feature of item being measured and follow all contours in the process. The glove shall not measure more than 12" from the tip of any one of the four fingers, through the ball pocket to the bottom edge or heel of gloves the gloves you're not measure more than 7 ¾" wide measured from the inside seam at base of first finger along base of other fingers, to the outside edge of little finger of the glove.

Rule 1.14 goes on to describe the specifications for the glove's webbing size and material, and the space between the glove's thumb and forefinger called the "crotch." Peters makes a special note in his memo that "There are a limited number of gloves in use that exceed these new measurements and you are put on notice that such gloves may not be used in professional championship games after May 5, 1972" (Peters, 1972).

The changes in the rules reflect a longstanding issue in the history of the baseball glove: Once the glove was adopted as a common piece of equipment, players experimented with bigger and bigger gloves to make catching easier. In the Giamatti Research Center at the National Baseball Hall of Fame and Museum, there is a clippings file dedicated to baseball gloves, and many of the images feature players using oversized mitts for a variety of reasons. A photo taken around 1930 shows a high school player from Newburyport, Massachusetts wearing a glove the size of a manhole cover. In an unattributed clipping from 1939 titled "Pardon My Glove!" Washington Senators first baseman Zeke Bonura holds up an illegal glove. The caption quotes Major League Baseball commissioner Kenesaw Mountain Landis complaining that "Some of the boys were building themselves lacrosse nets." That same year in an article from the *Greensboro (NC) Daily News*, rookie Reds pitcher Joe Orrell is shown with a mitt his manager claimed could be used "for a cushion when sitting on the bench. I don't even know if he could use it for that, it's so big." Orrell's explanation for using the glove is in keeping with some of the primary themes we've seen throughout the chapter. Adoption of and experimentation with the glove derives from two complementary motives: safety and competitive advantage. "I wanted something to hide my pitches," Orrell claims:

> Smart coaches who think they can catch my signals and tell what kind of pitch I'm going to throw will find out differently this year. Besides I've been wanting a glove for a long time that I could use to pick up ground

balls. I've had drives hit my legs long enough. I can knock them down with my new glove I really thought the glove was a little too long at first but I believe it's going to be all right after I get used to it. I'll have to wear it a while and get it adjusted to my hand.

(Horner, 1939)

Perhaps the most famous example of a player using a larger glove to his advantage was in 1960, when Orioles catcher Clint Courtney donned an oversized mitt "half again the size of a standard catcher's mitt" behind the plate in a game pitched by the Hall of Fame knuckle baller Hoyt Wilhelm (see Figure 1.10). For the first time in his career, Wilhelm pitched a complete game without a single passed ball (Lang, 1960).

Although the 1895 original rules specified that for fielders the glove not measure "in circumference around the palm of the hand not over fourteen inches," since the 1930s, the standard has been a glove no longer than 12 inches. But there are many players who violate that rule, and for the most part, Major League

Figure 1.10 **Clint Courtney with Bobby Thompson (1960).** (*Source*: The Baltimore Sun.)

Baseball defers to personal preference and common practice. However, periodically, the commissioner and the rules committee make an effort to enforce the standard. This was the case when Commissioner Landis lamented the "lacrosse nets" players were inventing, and the rules change in 1972 reflects a push to rein in longer glove lengths. That effort then gets revisited nearly 20 years later, when Major League Baseball announced (once again) that it would be measuring player's gloves to see if they conformed (Baseball Mitt Crackdown, 1990; Schultz, 1990). "Players can expect a crackdown on mammoth mitts this season" reported *USA Today* in the spring of 1990:

> Suspect gloves will be inspected to make sure they measure no more than 12 inches from the tip of the web to the heel. Said Joe Carter, . . .: "If they say they're going to check, I'll make sure my glove is 12 inches or less. That's the rules. I'll stay in the rules."

(Johnson, 1990)

And once again, the specter of slowing down the game appears as a counterargument for changing or re-enforcing a rule about the glove. In a 1990 Associated Press report Marty Springstead, supervisor of AL umpires acknowledged the potential for gamesmanship with the glove rule, when umpires had to carry tape measures and managers could challenge equipment twice per game. "We don't want glove checks to be some sort of tactic, something to disrupt the pitcher." Nevertheless, Springstead conceded, "I'm sure that if one manager makes a glove check, the other manager will, too. That's the nature of baseball" (National Baseball Hall of Fame and Museum. Clippings File "Baseball Gloves").

By far the biggest offenders of the glove size rules were outfielders, who typically wear the longest gloves on the field and need the extra length to snare fly balls on the run. Most outfielders wear a glove at least 12.75-inches long, and some, especially in the 1970s and 1980s would wear ones substantially longer. Joe Carter typically wore 14-inch glove, as did Brett Butler, but few, if any outfielders actually abided by the rule, and the glove manufacturers were happily complicit in skirting the size limit. In the wake of the 1972 rules crackdown, *The Sporting News* quotes an unnamed, but unapologetic representative of the sporting goods industry: "If a big glove is good then the players think an even bigger glove is better . . . we couldn't keep within the rules and not face a loss of business to the bigger glove" (Kaham, 1972).

Hence, in a curious wrinkle for a game defined by—and some might say obsessed by—the intricacy of its rules, for nearly a century, a sizable percentage of players broke the rules, simply by donning a glove. In 1990 *USA Today* estimated that perhaps 80 percent of outfielders were in violation. It comes as no surprise therefore—except the surprise at how long it took –that in 2017, Major League Baseball changed the rules to reflect the practice. Rule 3.06 (its new number) states that "the glove shall not measure more than *13 inches* from the tip of any one of the 4 fingers, through the ball pocket to the bottom edge or heel of glove."

What the question of the glove's size reveals is that, to evoke the historian Peter Morris once again, baseball really is a "game of inches." From the moment the glove appeared in the rules in 1895, to its most recent codification as a 13-inch piece of leather, we have managed to arrive in the present, and along the way, we have had the opportunity to consider the glove's emergence in a network of discourses about fair play, gender, and value, many of which are codified in the rules of baseball, and some of which are couched in terms of tradition, ritual, and beliefs. The intersection of rules and belief can be said to constitute one version of its history, but the episodes I have highlighted are by no means meant to exhaust the full story of the glove's evolution, development, and how it figures into a set of practices that contribute to its status as a culturally significant object. Instead, the way the glove has evolved as part of the game and the coextensive development of the rules points our way to a consideration of other aspects of the glove's existence, its status as a material object and its participation in a wide range of practices both on and off the field that give it its meaning. We have had occasion to look at how the glove shapes and is shaped by the rules of baseball, and we will have cause to return to the rules throughout the following chapters as a reminder of the gap that often exists between an object that has both a rule-bound existence and an existence rich with meanings rooted in everyday practices, routines, and beliefs. Let us now turn our attention to how the glove is shaped by and shapes those who use it, so that in turn we can come to grips with how it might come to embody something like meaning.

Notes

1 Since "Pioneer Baseball" is a typescript reproduction of McGunnigle's scrapbook, with some personal annotations thrown in, it is sometimes difficult to attribute the individual entries McGunnigle cites. Hence, I refer to the page numbers in the manuscript rather than to the original sources.

2 In a public forum to discuss the book *Moneyball*, my VTMSBL teammate, former Red Sox pitcher Bill Lee told the crowd, "When I first met Dave, he couldn't hit. He couldn't even hit water if he fell out of a boat."

2

MATERIAL

Having looked at some of the episodes in the history of the baseball glove, how are we to understand the glove as also having a material existence? As we saw in the previous chapter on the glove's history, seeing the evolution of the glove through the lens of the official rules of baseball might be a good place to start. In the essay, "How Can One Be a Sports Fan?" Pierre Bourdieu describes the significance of the rules for understanding the development of sports as codified practices with their own cultural specificity. "The autonomization of the field of sport is also accompanied by a process of rationalization intended," Bourdieu insists "to ensure predictability and calculability, beyond local differences and particularisms: the constitution of specific rules and of specialized governing bodies" (Bourdieu, 1999: 430) In terms of the baseball glove, one could almost write a book about how oddly specific these rules are, were it not for the fact that by 2017 they were already nearly the length of a book themselves (see Figure 2.1).

If you remember, the first rule regarding gloves appeared in 1895:

RULE 19. SECTION. 2. The catcher and first baseman are permitted to wear a glove or mitt of any size, shape or weight. All other players are restricted to the use of a glove or mitt weighing not over ten ounces, and measuring in circumference around the palm of the hand not over fourteen inches.

(Spalding Guide, 1895)

Over the course of the next 120 years, the rules governing the glove expanded. By the middle of the twentieth century, what once was a terse two sentences and 51 words has expanded to four paragraphs and 350 words. While the 1895 rules offered little guidance for fielders, and none at all for catchers and first basemen, the 1955 version of *The Official Rules of Baseball* specifies the length of the glove (12 inches), the material (leather), the design of the webbing (which "cannot be constructed of wound or wrapped lacing to make a net type of trap"), and the color (for pitchers, it had to be "uniform in color and cannot be white or gray").

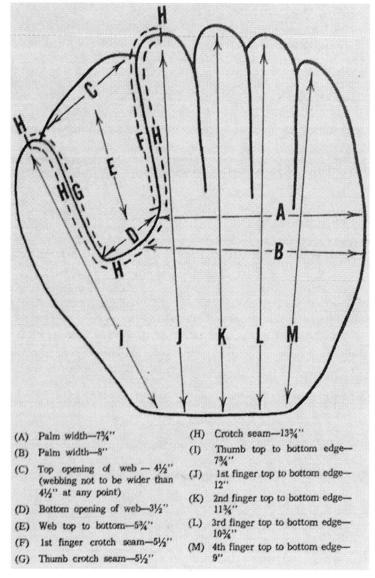

(A) Palm width—7¾"
(B) Palm width—8"
(C) Top opening of web — 4½" (webbing not to be wider than 4½" at any point)
(D) Bottom opening of web—3½"
(E) Web top to bottom—5¾"
(F) 1st finger crotch seam—5½"
(G) Thumb crotch seam—5½"
(H) Crotch seam—13¾"
(I) Thumb top to bottom edge—7¾"
(J) 1st finger top to bottom edge—12"
(K) 2nd finger top to bottom edge—11¾"
(L) 3rd finger top to bottom edge—10¾"
(M) 4th finger top to bottom edge—9"

Figure 2.1 **Dimensions of Fielder's Glove (2016).** (*Source:* Office of the Commissioner of Baseball.)

After another 60 years, the rules concerning gloves and mitts have ballooned once again, this time to 848 words covering size, weight, and material with separate rules for catchers, first basemen, pitchers, and fielders. The most recent version of the rules also covers such minutiae as "crotch opening," the placement of the measuring tape used to gauge the size of the glove, and a far more detailed description of the allowable color range: "The pitcher's glove may not, exclusive of piping, be white, gray, nor, in the judgment of an umpire, distracting in any manner. No fielder, regardless of position, may use a fielding glove that falls within a PANTONE® color set lighter than the current 14-series" (Office of the Commissioner of Baseball, 2017: 7–9).

I have chosen three representative examples of the rules regarding gloves from over a century of baseball, but one could fill many pages with the minute changes that appear from year to year. However, from the standpoint of a book about a specific cultural object, what is especially noteworthy about these rules is how intimate they are with the materiality of the glove in its three primary forms: catcher's mitt, first basemen's mitt, and fielder's glove. There is something both clinical and sensual about the descriptions of the thumb crotch and the exacting tactility of measuring the glove ("The tool or measuring tape shall be placed to contact the surface or feature of item being measured and follow all contours in the process"), and there is almost something mythic to the idea of a webbing that "shall not be enlarged, extended, or reinforced by any process or materials whatever" (Office of the Commissioner of Baseball, 2017: 8).

Although we have paid some attention to the way the Official Rules shape and are shaped by the history of the glove, just as the Spalding company's description of the history of the baseball glove held only tenuous connections to the complex and contradictory series of events and set of practices that form the cultural history of the baseball glove, the rule book definition of the glove is hardly the final word on the material reality of the glove as it is used both historically and in the contemporary game.

That said, the evolution of the glove and the rules that govern it offer a glimpse into the way that adaptation, innovations in design, and changes in custom and habit can condition the official discourse concerning a material object. "One important point to note," Peter Morris insists about baseball innovations "is how many revolve around the issue of competitiveness":

> Baseball's earliest players viewed baseball primarily as a recreation rather than as a competition, and although this changed quickly, many of the games rules and customs were much slower to change. This led to cycles in which an innovative player or manager found a strategy not covered by the rules but not deemed entirely sporting. New rules were introduced to eliminate or govern the new tactic; more new strategies were brought forward as a result of the new rule; new techniques emerged to counteract them, and so on until a compromise was reached.
>
> (Morris, 2010: xxiii)

The material life of a glove, its making and remaking, its shaping and reshaping speak to issues of design and ingenuity, ritual and belief, scientific principles, industrial practices, and conventional wisdom, but it also speaks to the evolving set of social negotiations regarding proper "sporting" practice of the game ultimately embodied in the rules. As was the case in the previous chapter, the questions I am asking about the glove's status as a material object necessarily overlap with other questions about the meaning and value of the glove, for no material object, particularly not one produced for sale in a global marketplace can be innocent of these issues. We have already seen how the development of the baseball glove overlaps with social issues in the purported connection between the use of a glove and the issue of a player's masculinity. But that social dynamic was always at odds with a countervailing need to gain competitive advantage as Peter Morris reminds us. From the late nineteenth century to the middle of the twentieth, a number of design innovations enhanced the glove's efficiency. As with the introduction of the glove, these changes were not always met with praise, gratitude, or admiration, and were often as likely to be met with ridicule and claims they violated the traditions of the game.

Hence, the first question I have about the glove's material existence is also a historical one: How does the glove come to exist in its present form? By way of answering this question, here is an experiment to try: Take a baseball or a tennis ball in one hand and throw it—gently—into your other hand. Watch what the receiving hand does as it catches the ball. Notice the position of the fingers and the shape of the palm. Where does the ball fit in your hand?

Now, put a modern-day baseball or softball glove on your catching hand, and throw the ball into it. Imagine you could see through the glove at your hand inside. What would it look like? What position are the fingers in as they catch the ball? Are they straight or bent? How about the palm?

In the barehanded version of this experiment, the ball is caught in the palm of your hand, and the fingers curl around it from the top while the thumb curls up from the bottom. In the second experiment, the motion of the hand and the position of the ball is altogether different. Your fingers are more rigid and tend to stay close together. Your thumb and forefingers come together not from opposite poles but from more like a 45-degree angle, and the ball when it is caught tends to sit between the thumb and index finger, perhaps not touching the hand at all.

The evolution of the design of the glove reflects the differences our experiment identifies. Remember, originally, gloves were fingerless affairs, designed to pad and protect the palm from the impact of the ball. This padding allowed the fingers to do what they do naturally when catching a ball—bend at the knuckles to grip and then throw. However, once gloves with padded fingers came to the fore, although they succeeded in protecting the player's digits they often failed from a design perspective to efficiently catch a ball. A look at these gloves might explain why—with their large padded fingers and thumb, they restricted the ability of the player to bend their fingers around the ball. The result was akin to a leather pillow that required the assistance of the other hand to make an effective catch.

In the preface to their 2013 collection *Design Anthropology*, Wendy Gunn, Ton Otto, and Rachel Charlotte Smith argue that understanding design evolution is essentially to take an anthropological approach to objects. First, design is historical: "Design practices attempt to make connections (albeit partial) between past, present, and future." Second, focusing on design forces the anthropologist to countenance how complex and evolving social forces are embodied in material reality. "Practitioners of design anthropology," they argue, "follow dynamic situations and social relations and are concerned with how people perceive, create, and transform their environments through their everyday activities" (Gunn et al., 2013: xiii).

Anthropologists and theorists who study material culture are curious about questions of functionality and embodiment, what objects do, how things are made and used and how those uses reshape the makers (Boradkar, 2010). Typically, we believe that an object evolves due to a desire to improve its function, but as Beth Preston reminds us, the term "function" can have ideological implications: "Function is a normative concept. We often talk about things malfunctioning, and have very definite ideas about what they are supposed to have the capacity or disposition to do even in cases where they clearly are not so capable or so disposed" (Preston, 2000: 26). The function of an object is always historically determined. Certain objects "work" at certain moments by virtue of a collective set of practices and beliefs about their utility. Take an object out of its historical context, and you take away that object's functionality. To take an extreme example, a person living in the middle ages would likely have no epistemological capacity to make use of an iPhone, even if they had a charger and WiFi. The sheer amount of background knowledge necessary to make it work simply would not compute. Hence, the functionality of an object depends on a historical chain of previously functioning items. "Proper functions are acquired or lost not by individual existing things but by lineages of things," Preston argues:

> The key question to ask here is: Is this sort of thing now being reproduced because previous things of that sort successfully performed the function in question? If the answer is "yes," then this function is a proper function, regardless of what the original proper function of the thing may have been (or may still be, since it may be retained alongside the new proper function).

(Preston, 2000: 31)

Society, therefore, may to a very great extent be understood in terms of a constellation of the interactions between people and their objects. "Social structures are defined in large part by the prescribed material culture they involve. More specifically, it is the proper functions of the objects making up the material culture which define these structures at the most basic level" (Preston, 2000: 41).

Preston's argument about functionality appears in the influential collection, *Matter, Materiality, and Modern Culture*, published in 2000, and Preston's co-contributors amplify her point about the mutually co-determining nature of human-object interactions. The editor of the volume, P.M. Graves-Brown argues that chief among the objects transformed by human history is our own selves. It is worth remembering, Graves-Brown argues "that the first human artefact is the human body itself, and that action by and upon the body is the core to understanding our culture" (Graves-Brown, 2000: 3).

For his part, Bruno Latour sees the interplay between human and objects as a complicated dynamic of intersecting forces far more complicated than what Ingold (2000, 2010) called the hylomorphic interplay between form-givers and objects:

> A dialectic, then? If you like, but only on condition that we abandon the mad idea that the subject is posed in its opposition to the object, for there are neither subjects nor objects, neither in the beginning – mythical– nor in the end – equally mythical. Circulations, sequences, transfers, translations, displacements, crystallisations there are many motions, certainly, but not a single one of them, perhaps, that resembles a contradiction.

> (Latour, 2000: 10)

The baseball glove, which historically developed in relationship to an evolving set of ideas about masculinity, fair play, rules, and gamesmanship, while at the same time paralleling the development of the game's equipment as a set of saleable commodities, embodies Latour's contradictions. Many of the glove's design innovations are a response to the needs of players in the field, but they are also part of an economy that constantly needs to market and promote new and improved items for sale (see Breakout Box 2.1). From an anthropological perspective, what is perhaps most fascinating about the baseball glove given the push of these forces, is how *slowly* it develops and how long certain design innovations stick, perhaps as a result of the countervailing weight of tradition, but there is also no underestimating the power of ridicule in the game, and from the origin of the glove and the putative—although likely apocryphal—aspersions cast on player's manhood, each advance in glove design has come with its fair share of detractors.

Perhaps the most significant of the early changes to glove design was the one devised by Bill Doak, a Saint Louis Cardinals pitcher and one of the last players grandfathered into the rules to legally throw a spitball after it was banned in 1920. The year before the spitball rule went into effect, Doak made his other lasting contribution to the game: he introduced the idea of a piece of webbing between the thumb and index finger of the glove (see Figure 2.2). Now, instead of catching a ball in the palm, the player was able to make a catch with the ball hitting a pocket formed by the webbing and two fingers—an easier and less painful

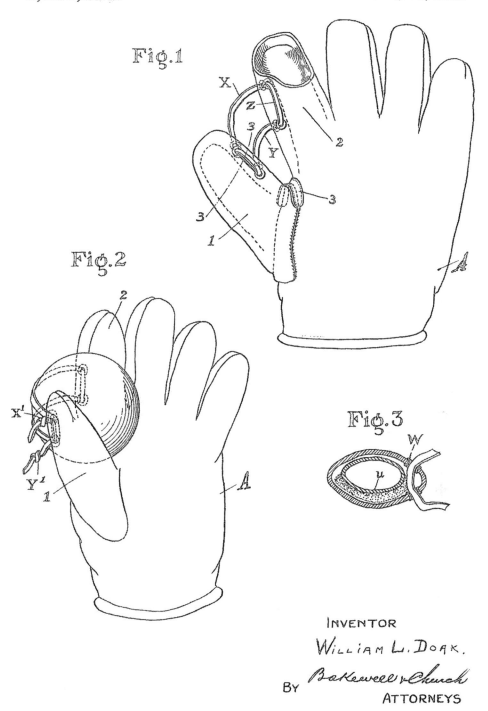

W. L. DOAK.

FIELDER'S GLOVE.

APPLICATION FILED APR. 18, 1921.

1,426,824.

Patented Aug. 22, 1922.

Fig.1

Fig.2

Fig.3

INVENTOR

WILLIAM L. DOAK.

BY Bakewell & Church

ATTORNEYS

Figure 2.2 **William L. Doak, "Fielder's Glove" (1922). Patent 1,426,824.** (*Source*: Google Patents.)

way to field the ball. By adding the webbing, Doak claimed, and "by enlarging the thumb, bringing it up even with the first finger, a larger pocket is formed and many balls are caught on the very tips of the thumb and first finger" (quoted in Steinberg, 2004). Doak sold his patented idea to Rawlings who began selling this new "Premier Players' Glove" in 1920. Over the next few decades, although a number of innovations improved on the glove, like putting lacing between the fingers so they could close simultaneously, Doak's idea proved so influential that his Premier Players' model remained in the Rawlings catalog for nearly 40 years.

Nevertheless, the glove still had significant design flaws. In *Glove Affairs*, Noah Liberman explains:

> Take a look at it and note all of the features that appear to make it *hard* to catch the ball. There's the thick, round, stiff, thumb and the thick round, stubby pinkie. There's the heavy padding at the heel. There's no hinge. There's a small pocket, the result of so much padding and no hinge. There are no laces between the fingers. In 1943, 40 years after Wilbur Wright's flight, American pilots were flying jets and American professionals were still catching balls with pillows. You did your best to catch the ball in the palm then. The rolled-lace web would snare the ball too, but it didn't allow for the quickest return throw. This was not optimal design.

> (Liberman, 2003: 24)

In 1957, however, Wilson introduced a leap forward in design every bit as significant as Bill Doak's webbing, the A2000. Its innovations were immediately apparent. "Analyze the A2000," Liberman insists. "The A2000 doesn't look like a human hand. It took almost 90 years for ballplayers and glovemakers to shake off the belief, or was it the instinct? That the glove must look like the hand" (Liberman, 2003: 25).

The A2000 solved many of the Doak model deficiencies. It had a hinge to help the glove snap closed automatically around a deeply formed Grip-Tite pocket, "the widest and deepest in the game to help you catch every ball 'for keeps'" claimed a May 1963 two-page ad in *Boys' Life* ("Your hand has no such thing," Liberman explains; "it doesn't need it, because the thumb and fingers move brilliantly on their own"). It also had a substantial "Barrel-Stave" web design, which, according to another ad "gives you inches more reach—helps you make leaping grabs and one-handed stabs like famous big league 'glove men'!" (see Figure 2.3, [*Boys' Life*, April, 1962]). And, as Steve Rushin writes in *The 34-Ton Bat*, as a piece of product design, the A2000 caused writers and baseball fans alike to wax rhapsodic:

> Many have tried, but it's nearly impossible to overstate what an object of beauty the A2000 is, with its near perfect symmetry and a golden-brown glaze that makes many models resemble a Thanksgiving turkey, fresh from

Figure 2.3 Wilson A2000 Advertisement, *Boys' Life* (April 1962).

the oven. "It's not just a baseball glove," Esquire magazine declared fifty years after the A2K's introduction, "it's the single greatest piece of sporting equipment ever built." To sportswriter Dave Kindred, who kept an A2000 on his desktop computer as a muse, 'the Wilson A2000 is a masterpiece of man's creative urge'."

(Rushin, 2013: 104)

My Wilson A-2000 is only the 3rd glove I've used in 67 years of baseball and softball, although I was given a first baseman's mitt and use the team's catcher's mitt. I bought my A-2000 in Vermont in the eighties for softball when a glove from high school/college died. It's still like new because my duties in the senior league have been mostly behind the plate. It probably came from Charlie's in Waterbury – a specialty shop that has long since gone.

(VTMSBL player)

The introduction of the A2000 was followed quickly by Rawlings' XPG in 1958 and the famous Heart of the Hide in 1961. For more than 60 years, Rawlings gloves were designed by the father and son team of Harry and Rollie Latina (see Figure 2.4). Harry ("Doc") worked for Rawlings from 1922 to 1961 and after he retired, Rollie ("The Glove Doctor") continued designing gloves until 1983. Between the two of them, they were responsible for some of the most distinctive design innovations in the history of the glove including the Trap-Eze web, the Snap-Back wrist band, The Hold-Ster Finger slot, and the Basket Weave web to name just a few.

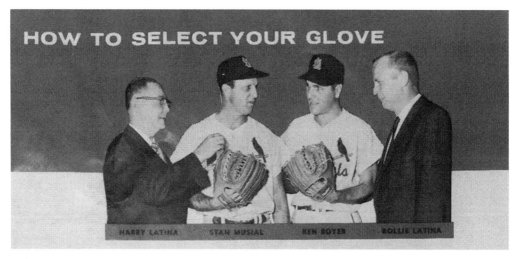

Figure 2.4 **Harry and Rollie Latina (with Stan Musial and Ken Boyer), (1961).** (*Source*: Part of an advertisement for Rawlings baseball gloves. National Baseball Hall of Fame.)

Breakout Box 2.1: Practicing Anthropology: Find a Patent

As we have seen, gloves have evolved a great deal over the 150 years since they were first introduced to the game as basic leather palms. Some of the innovations in glove evolution have been transformative—Bill Doak's webbing, Wilson's Design for the A2000, and Rawlings' introduction of the Ed-U-Cated Heel have had a major impact on how a glove performs its functions.

This evolution can be traced over time not only in company advertisements, newspaper clippings, game footage, and ephemera, but also in the records of the various patents issued for glove designs. These patents are an important part of the biography of the glove. They represent two parallel discourses. On the one hand, they reflect a set of beliefs about how best to play the game, and at the same time, according to the theories of design anthropology, they reflect a continuing interaction between the material existence of the glove and the ideological forces at work in consumer capitalism involving innovation, marketing, and design.

In order to see these forces at play, find a glove patent. A patent is a revealing object of material culture history (see Figure 2.5). It is a legal document typically consists of two parts, a diagram of the invention and a rationale for what makes the invention significantly innovative. At the same time that a patent is announcing something new, a patent rationale is necessarily a dialogue with the past, citing previous patents that the current innovation supersedes. Google has a patent database. For an assignment, use it to research a glove patent application. What innovation does your patent make? How does it affect the function of the glove? Why is this innovation significant (or why not)? Is it in use today?

What patents or previous innovations does your patent reference? How—if at all—has your patent been superseded? Finally, what does your patent tell you about the larger concerns of the game at the moment when the innovation was introduced? What sets of practices does it assume or overthrow? Share your observations with your classmates. Taken altogether, what picture of the glove's evolution emerges from these? What might these developments tell you about the concerns about the glove's design from the standpoint of players? What about for producers of a commodity offered for sale to consumers? Ask your students to write a biography of the glove featured in the patent. What story does it tell?

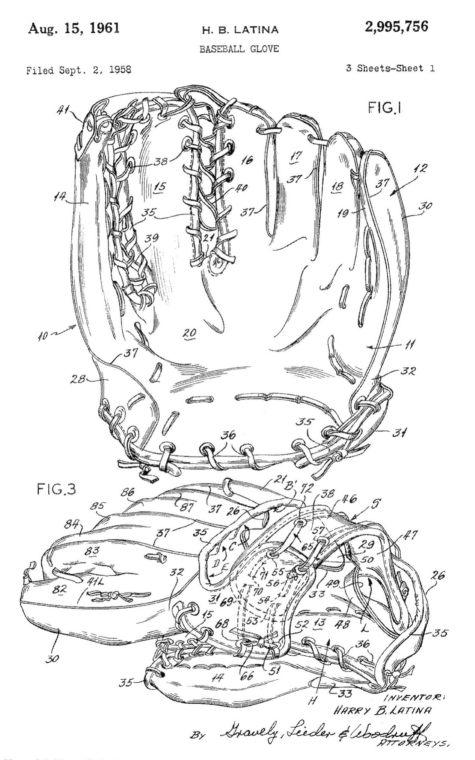

Figure 2.5 **Harry B. Latina "Baseball Glove" (1961). Patent 2,995,756.** (*Source*: Google Patents.)

The Wilson A2000 and its nearest competitor, the Rawlings Heart of the Hide so successfully transformed the act of catching that these models effectively set the template for modern baseball gloves, and both models are on the market to this day. The influential French anthropologist Marcel Mauss once wrote that the human body was "the first and most natural technical object of man, and at the same time his technical tool" (Mauss, 1973: 75), but with the A2000 and the Latinas' designs, glove manufacturers sought to improve on the efficiency of the body and its ability to catch a baseball. What made these models so successful is that they managed to out-do the design of perhaps human beings' most distinctive feature beyond our big brains and the capacity for abstract reasoning and metacognition: the human hand.

From a design perspective, the hand is a marvel, capable of the fine work of writing the first draft of this book by grasping a pen and the second draft by tapping the letters on a keyboard; deft and dexterous enough for surgery or piano playing—the preservation and sustaining of life physically and spiritually through medicine and culture. "Of all the human limbs," the sociologist Richard Sennett claims: "the hands make the most varied movements, movements that can be controlled at will. Science has sought to show how these motions, plus the hand's varied ways of gripping and the sense of touch, affect how we think" (Sennett, 2008: 149). The hand has proved a remarkable adaptation from the standpoint of evolution. Whereas prior to the development of evolutionary theory, Sennett claims, scientists "believed the hand came from God the Creator perfectly designed, a fit-for-purpose limb like all of his works," Charles Darwin helped change that notion arguing that the hand developed in conjunction with the expansion of our brain's ability to process information. "With greater brain capacity, our human ancestors learned how to hold things in their hands, to think about what they held, and eventually to shape the things held; man-apes could make tools, humans make culture" (Sennett, 2008: 150).

For our hunter ancestors, the hand helped us in everything from gripping stones and projectiles to hurl at our prey, to grasping and holding the prey as we carry it home, to pulling the last bit of tasty flesh from the bones. It proves no less useful for the herbivore gatherers, since our fingers are sensitive enough to pick small fruits from a bush and distinguish between a wild blackberry and a thorn with just the slightest pressure. Hands allow us to consume more calories more efficiently; they help us construct more effective domiciles; and they construct warmer and more airtight covering and clothing. But their dexterity and sensitivity mean that our hands are inadequately suited to catching a thrown or batted sphere. Fingers bend and break; the bones and tendons of our palms are only barely padded by skin and muscle. Our hand's increased sensitivity comes courtesy of densely packed and highly specialized nerve endings—and when those nerves are stimulated by a projectile moving at speeds up to 100 miles per hour, they hurt! The design innovations of the baseball glove help minimize that pain and overcome the hand's inefficiencies. Today's glove manages to outthink the design of the hand. And indeed, the baseball glove forces the hand in the act of catching to remake itself as an extension of the glove.

We make the objects we find useful for living in the world but these objects also make and shape us. As the influential anthropologist Daniel Miller reminds us, "It is clear, that in material culture we are concerned at least as much with how things make people as the other way around" (Miller, 2010: 43). This mutual shaping takes place in a variety of registers and for a variety of reasons, some more direct, some less so. At the same time, when an object doesn't function properly, it may also be the case that the user hasn't adapted him or herself to the possibilities either embodied or latent in an object's design. An object that doesn't function as anticipated is ripe for redesign, but then again, it may be that the human users need to be retrained to the demands embodied by their material objects. To return to our extreme example of the iPhone, now a decade after its introduction we have come to understand that beyond all of the wondrous access to information it provides, our smartphones also serve as addiction devices, delivering tiny doses of dopamine with each alert or text, rendering it increasingly difficult for us to resist the urge to reach for our phone while in class, or having dinner with our children, or driving (Richtel, 2015).

With respect to the baseball glove, players have been shaped by the object at the same time the object's material design has evolved. This evolution is not simply deterministic. The glove is also a specialized object. A catcher's mitt is round, designed to receive pitches and absorb the maximum impact of a pitchers' top velocity. A first basemen's mitt is elongated and designed to scoop balls from the dirt and snag balls right at the fingertips, because milliseconds count as a runner is trying to beat a throw to first. Even fielders' gloves, which at first glance might look essentially the same, bear a number of differences when held up to scrutiny. Second basemen and shortstop gloves tend to be smaller with a shallower pocket so that the middle-infielders can transfer a ball from the glove to the throwing hand as quickly as possible when turning a double play. Outfielders have longer gloves to help catching fly balls. Pitchers almost always wear gloves with a closed webbing to hide the ball when on the mound to disguise their grip and hide the next pitch from the opposing batter.

There is often a mutually self-determining relationship between the glove and the body of the player. While it is not always the case that second-basemen are small and quick, catchers are stocky and slow, and first basemen are massive and have limited mobility, it is the case that almost without exception, second basemen, shortstops, third basemen and catchers throw with their right and catch with their left; first basemen throw with their left and catch with their right; pitchers and outfielders can be either-handed. In Major League Baseball, when Cubs left-hander Anthony Rizzo took third base for an inning on August 22, 2017, it was the first time a major-league lefty had played the position in 20 years, and the first time a Cub had done so since 1895 (Sharkey-Gotlieb, 2017). And although there have been a number of lefties who have penciled in as shortstops to get an at bat in the lineup, the last lefty to get a fielding chance at the position was Hal Chase in 1910. The reasons for this are utterly pragmatic; a lefty playing one of the non-first base infield positions has to contort his body in an awkward manner to make a throw to first, throwing against the usual momentum of his body.

The reasons for why there are few lefty catchers are somewhat less clear. A *New York Times* article in 2009 interviewed professional players and managers players to find an answer, but wound up concluding that "left-handed catchers are effectively extinct — for reasons on which there is bizarrely little consensus." There has not been a lefty Major League catcher since Benny Distefano played for the Pirates in 1989 (Schwarz, 2009). The way that the game demands certain body types and a specific "handedness" for certain positions has an impact on the biography of the glove. Many is the Little League coach with a young left hander who wants to play catcher who realizes that the gear bag provided by the league only contains a righty catcher's mitt. I encountered this first hand with my youngest son, who is left-handed and wanted to play catcher. Fortunately, I was able to find a lefty catcher's mitt for very little money. When I bragged to a friend of mine who works as a professional scout about the deal I found, he responded by teasing me, "You're doing something wrong if you can't find a lefty catcher's mitt on sale." What his jibe reveals is the connection between design, history, and practice. The evolution of the game and the parallel evolution of the glove means that certain gloves are for certain players with certain types of bodies: It's an anomaly for a lefty to wear a catcher's mitt. But at the intersection of design, history, and practices emerges another organizing framework, value. A left-handed catcher's mitt isn't worth much—or as much—as a glove designed for someone better suited to the position. It seems like an obvious observation, but it gets at the heart of the relationship between design and anthropology: Making things—and more importantly, the way things are made, the form they take and the evolution they undergo—reveals a lot about cultural and economic value. As Ann Balsamo argues, "Through the practices of designing, cultural beliefs are materially reproduced, identities are established, and social relations are codified. Culture is both a resource for, and an outcome of, the design process" (Balsamo, 2011: 11). Design is a way of knowing the world, and the evolution of a piece of equipment is a form of knowledge production (Otto and Smith, 2013) as much as it is a commodity production. To a very real extent, a catcher's mitt makes the catcher and the second baseman's glove makes the second baseman as much as the other way around.

My first glove was a 1970's youth Wilson that was left handed, blue, and a hand-me-down from my older brother. I was probably 4 or 5 and my brother was ready for a new glove for the peanut league season. At the time I never questioned if there was another option as this was the glove I was handed. My brother, being the ravenous baseball player would hound me nightly to catch him in the back yard, field behind the barns or where ever he created a new ball field. I would say no until my demands were met or the bribery payed. In the end I was a lefty like him even though today I do all other tasks right handed.

(VTMSBL player)

Makers and Shapers—in Their Own Words—Part 1

The question of how the glove shapes the game and its players leads necessarily to the question of how a glove is made and what happens to it in the process of going from raw material to a useful and usable piece of equipment (see Breakout Box 2.2). From the standpoint of industrial production, a baseball glove is a somewhat idiosyncratic object, but one in keeping with much of the reality of the global production of commodities. In Pietra Rivoli's book, *The Travels of a T-shirt in the Global Economy* (2009) Rivoli, an economist, describes the passage of a T-shirt from raw material—the cotton grown on a farm in Smyer, Texas—to the cotton's processing and the production of the T-shirt in a factory in China, to its sale in a store in the United States, to its donation at the Salvation Army and ultimately to its sale once more by East African entrepreneurs.

The passage of a baseball glove from raw material to consumer is similarly complex. Most gloves are made from steerhide, which generally comes from throughout the United States, but typically from the Midwest and Southwest. Those hides are processed in tanneries in Milwaukee and Chicago, where the hair is removed, soaked, and spun in a variety of chemical baths and dyes to give them their durability and color, then shaved to the thickness suitable for use. Those tanned hides are then shipped to factories—predominately overseas—where the process of glove manufacturing takes place. Those gloves are then sold, many to the US market. If the glove is an heirloom or one of personal significance, it will likely stay in the States. If it is donated, however, it could end up in the Dominican Republic or in Cuba. When I was in Cuba with a youth baseball team, there were gloves from many different manufacturers (see Figure 1.1), but the only new glove I saw during my whole visit was a Dong Hyuk model from China, which because of the embargo on US goods, was likely one of the few brands eligible for sale in the country.

For an object as uniquely associated with America as a baseball glove, today, whatever the name on the label, most of the production of gloves takes place overseas. Rawlings will still produce a few of their high-end custom gloves in St. Louis, where they are headquartered, and up until just a few years ago, Louisville Slugger was producing a line of Evolution gloves that bore a "Made in the USA" label, but no longer. Most glove manufacturing for the US market is done in China and the Philippines with some in Mexico, Korea, and Indonesia. Manufacturing a glove is a complicated, multipart process, and there are a number of videos and articles that that show how it is made (Berlow, 2007; How It's Made Baseball Gloves, 2015). The process involves cutting the leather with a die, aligning and assembling the shell and lining, assembling the web and affixing it to the glove, and lacing and stitching the glove. In addition, at many of the steps along the way, the glove needs to be turned inside or right-side out, adhesives need to be applied to various parts of the glove, and labels, tags, and embroidery need to be applied. Finally, the glove needs to be coated in a glove petroleum and have the finger stalls formed.

Much of this work has to be done by hand. A steerhide is an irregularly shaped object; so too are the dies used to cut the shape of the glove. These have to be positioned by hand (see Figure 2.6). Likewise, because gloves come in multiple sizes and configurations, the stitching and lacing all generally require a human being. This is a labor-intensive process, and one that is expensive in the United States. Hence, most glove manufacturers have moved their operations offshore. When one considers—as I do in the next chapter—the rhetoric of "craftsmanship" that the glove manufacturers use in their marketing campaigns, we should remember that this rhetoric stands in for a complex history of the movement of labor and manufacturing around the world.

The predominant exception[1] to the end of glove manufacturing in the United States is the Nokona company in Nocona, Texas (there's a reason for the two different spellings). Nocona sits about an hour and 45 minutes northwest of Dallas in the Texas Hill country, a rolling, beautiful, and surprisingly green part of the state. It is also a profoundly conservative part of the country. Montague County, in which Nocona sits, voted for Trump 87.5 percent in 2016 (2016 Texas Presidential Election Results), and when I stopped for breakfast near the Nokona factory, a giant Trump–Pence poster covered the window of the diner, along with a sign advising patrons how to discharge their firearms responsibly should they need to do so on the premises (which weren't much bigger than my faculty office).

Whereas Nocona used to be something of a hub for leather goods, including a number of belt makers, today, the most noteworthy business in the town is the Nokona glove factory, which started manufacturing ball gloves in 1934. The company manufactures high end gloves (the entry-level Classic Walnut model

Figure 2.6 **Rob Storey with a steer side (2016), Nokona factory, Nocona, TX.** (*Source*: Photo by David Jenemann.)

starts at $290 on their website), about which Nolan Ryan once said: "My first glove was a Nokona. One of my favorite childhood memories was going down to Alvin Hardware with my Dad, and picking it out. The high quality of these gloves is what today's top players need, and they're the gloves I've chosen for my grandkids" ("Nokona," n.d.). That said, while the company cultivates young players, it does not pursue standard endorsement contracts. Rob Storey is the Executive Vice President of the Nokona company, and he walked me through the company's history and some of the business. What follows are some of the highlights of our time together.

DAVID JENEMANN: *You're known for some of your distinctive leathers.*
ROB STOREY: Our leather comes in almost all sizes, as opposed to hides or skin. Predominantly out of Milwaukee. Some out of Chicago, and then our kangaroo comes from Australia . . . There's three tanneries in Milwaukee that we use, and then there's one in Chicago. Horween, a big company. We go to the tanneries probably every two years. We catch up with what's new, see if we can see any inspiration from other industries, because one thing you'll notice about our gloves, a lot of the times, is they don't look like our competitors', because we're not going to go out and basically use black or conventional tan. We like to specialize with our leather, so we use buffalo. We use kangaroo, and then a lot of different types of cow hides. We'll walk through a tannery. The tannery may be serving the furniture industry, the

footwear industry, the handbag industry. You name it, and we may see some leather that's probably maybe better suited for them, but we think, "What would that look like in a ball glove?"

DJ: *Has there been a memorable instance where you said, "Oh my gosh, we have to use this in a glove?"*

RS: Well, let me give you an example of something that not myself, but my dad did. This leather is known as walnut. That's kind of our classic. That came out of the late '70s, and I tell people today, when I was working here in high school and then go out in college in '82, and came back, we had the Nocona Boot Company in town. We had the Nocona belt company, Brazos Joe Belt Company, just all leather goods, two or three saddle makers, ourself, Motley's Leather. All of these leather manufacturers. At the time, it wasn't unusual to go to lunch and see a leather salesman. Normally, we would see a leather salesman two or three days a week. These guys would come to Nocona to see Nocona boot, because they were a very large company.

That was the prime reason for being here, but then they could pick up a little side business coming to us. In the late '70s, early '80s, we had the urban cowboy phase. Cowboy boots just became huge. This particular type of leather, we call walnut, it's a crunch leather. It became a fad type of leather in the western boot industry. Everybody wanted that look. All the tanneries geared up and were just making hundreds of thousands of feet of this stuff. Like most fads, when it died, it just died with a thud.

The leather guys would come to Dad and were like, "Hey, I've got 80,000 feet of this that we overran." Let's say today we pay about $4 a foot. At the time, we might have been paying $3. He said, "I've got to get rid of it. I'll give it to you for a buck-fifty." At the time, in the late '70s, early '80s, we were still very, very much under pressure from imports, because the importation of ball gloves started in the early '60s. By the late '70s, our business, we were probably down to less than 5,000 gloves a year.

The upside to it was that our football business, being helmets, shoulder pads, all that, was going great guns. Through the years, that always seemed to kind of happen. When one line would be down, the other one would be up. Dad says, "Okay. A buck-50 leather, that's going to help us overcome a little bit of the disparity. It's kind of weird looking. It doesn't look like a traditional leather. We'll give it a shot." So he did, and people started saying, "Hey, that's different. I like it." At one time, there early on, we were running probably five different colors of a crunch leather. Walnut, tan, what we call banana tan, gray, red and blue. That's an example of us adopting something from another industry that has become our mainstay. The walnut is our staple leather, so to speak now.

Figure 2.7 **Gloves ready for lacing (2016), Nokona factory, Nocona, TX.** (*Source*: Photo by David Jenemann.)

DJ: *Tell me about the Indian Head icon* (see Figure 2.7) *and the name, "Nokona."*

RS: Okay. Nokona is a Comanche Indian word. Our town is named after a Comanche Indian chief named Peta Nocona, P-E-T-A. I always say there's a little bit of irony in that, because we're using leather. Peta Nocona was born in 1820, probably either up in Oklahoma, which was then known as Indian territory, or probably in the West Texas Palo Duro Canyon area. His significance to our history going forward is that he was the person that went on a raid back in 1836 that captured a few white people, one of them being a little nine-year-old girl. Her name was Cynthia Ann Parker. In Texas, she's kind of legendary, because she was a young white girl that was captured and lived the rest of her life with the Comanches.

The greater significance is that seven or eight years after she was captured, she married her captor, Peta Nocona. Their first son was born, and his name was Quanah. Quanah, among the Comanches, was the last great chief of the Comanches, and was very much a salesman, a showman, a promoter, and ultimately was the one that was responsible for getting the Comanches to move back to the reservation, where they ultimately knew they had to go. He was, like I said, such a promoter. He was such a showman and became so anglicized and wore the white man's clothes, that even in his 60s, he was traveling with Teddy Roosevelt, the president, on hunting expeditions and hanging out in Washington with all the white guys. He later adopted his mom's last name, the English name of Parker, so he became Quanah Parker. There's a town 100 miles west of here called Quana.

The K itself, when our company first started, we were called Nocona Leather Goods, because we were making wallets. N-O-C-O, even up until 2010, our corporate name was still N-O-C-O-N-A Athletic Goods. When my granddad made our first glove in 1934, he wanted to trademark N-O-C-O-N-A as a standalone word, because he would see our competitors. Rawlings would use only Rawlings. Wilson would use only Wilson. Nobody would ever put the sporting goods out there, so a lot of times, they would just use one word.

Big Bob, as we call him, my granddad, he contacted the trademark office in DC and told him he wanted N-O-C-O-N-A. They sent him a refusal letter, saying you can't, because there's an incorporated city in Texas. Being quick on his feet, he said that wasn't going to stop him. He said, "We're just going to change the spelling to K, and we'll tell everybody that's how the Indians spelled it." He probably never knew that he wasn't wrong. Well, in this book [*Empire of the Summer Moon*, by Sam Gwynn] which was very well done and very well researched, we find that there's five accepted spellings for Peta Nocona. N-O-C-O-N-A, N-O-C-O-N-I, N-A-C-O-N-A, N-A-K-O-N-A, and N-O-K-O-N-A. As I tell people, my granddad probably didn't know. He passed away in 1980, but he wasn't incorrect. That was one of the accepted spellings.

DJ: *Tell me about the new logo, which abstracts the Native American figure, doesn't it?*

RS: That is one of the good answers. It's a baseball diamond with stands. It's an American flag. It's whatever anybody wants it to be. Any time that you rebrand, you always have the Coke debacle from years ago in mind. To this day, I still wonder why multi-billion-dollar companies rebrand and even change their name. For 2017, which we're in that season already, we've got three basic looks. We've got what's called the modern. That would appeal more to kids. Then we've got the classic, which is with the Indian head. You'll see it in some of our product. Then we have another, that's going back to your glove, your newer glove. If somebody wants to order, and we've got some dealers that didn't want to gravitate towards this. There's a couple of internet dealers that can give us the volume, where we'll go back and make it the way we did two years ago. A good marketing manager would say, "That's stupid. You take one, and you live with it." There have been some people that loved it. There's been people that have hated it, and then people in the middle. I think it's done very well. That being said, we're still a very small piece of the pie when it comes to ball gloves. I've understood that maybe four and a half million gloves are sold annually in the United States. When we're selling 20,000 to 30,000 of those, we're just a drop in the bucket, but we like to think that we're, if you look at the whole market as a pyramid, we like to think we're right at the very top as far as quality and acceptance in the market. People, if they want a really, really good glove and they're willing the pay for it, they go to Nokona.

DJ: *You don't do endorsements anymore, but you used to . . .*

RS: The heyday of our endorsing was in the late '40s, early '50s. At the time, the AA team for the Brooklyn Dodgers was the Fort Worth Cats down here in Fort Worth. My granddad was a good friend with the general manager and owner down there. Obviously they played in this area, and would play in Oklahoma City a lot. As the bus carrying the players would come up US-81, 15 miles west of here on the way to Oklahoma City, they'd just divert over here. The whole Cats team would get out, and my granddad would give them all a free ball glove. Back in the '50s, two gloves was kind of the going rate for a glove contract. In the '48, '49 era, probably every player for the Fort Worth Cats were Nokona endorsees. Then they would go into the big leagues, Carl Ursin, Chico Carasquale, Don Hoke, Jim Lemon, Dick Williams. All those guys who were Nokona endorsees, because of the earlier affiliation.

DJ: *Where do you think that the industry is going?*

RS: I don't see any huge change one way or the other as far as our industry, related to the game of baseball. As goes baseball, so goes our industry. Our industry also, we're not just a baseball glove company. We're a fast pitch company, and that's a big part of what we do, because fast pitch baseball is so huge with girls in college programs, related back to Title IX regulations and quality of sports and things like that.

In the '70s, we were making very few gloves. In the '80s, trends turned a little bit over to softball, but particularly–and the reason I remember it is because my uncle passed away. He was running the company in '91. For whatever reason, they put me in charge of the company. When I was 31, I became the president of the company. My dad was still on board. He had been with the company 50 years at the time. For some reason, I don't know, he either took it on himself or we discussed it. We started designing some new models more related to adult softball. We went from a company making 20,000 glove a year to a company making 50,000 gloves. We were making a ton of ball gloves, all pretty much focused towards the adult softball market. During the '90s, there was a huge rise in amateur softball. I remember being in Washington DC for something, probably with one of my kids on a scout trip or something. Every park after 5:00 would have coed softball.

Along with those were what we call the beer leagues that were associated with the local bar. They bought the t-shirts. They all ended up in the bar after the games, and so our sales went up. Then about 2000, the adult softball market dries up, goes away. To this day, people in our industry still don't know why . . . We were huge in softball, but we had very little presence in baseball. We started recognizing this in 2000 or so. 2001, we decided hey, we need to get back into not only baseball, but really start concentrating more on fast pitch. During that 2000 to 2010 era, our baseball gloves started coming back, but in particular our fast pitch softball gloves. We have one of our fast pitch catchers that's probably still one of the top catchers' mitts in girls' softball.

Early on what we found was that daddies, even though they could be as serious about little girls playing softball as they could little boys playing Little League baseball, they still weren't willing to spend on the little girl like they would the little boy. That's slowly changing, but our baseball business now dominates what we do, with fast pitch being number two, and then adult softball being kind of the low man on the totem pole.

DJ: *Why do you make baseball gloves?*

RS: I wish I could find the clip. There is a clip from, I think it's the brother with AC/DC, the one of them who has gotten got dementia recently [Malcolm Young, who died in November 2017]. They said, "What would you do if you weren't a rock star?" Over a three or four second period, you could see his face go. He says, "I don't know. It's all I've ever done." He was sad about it, because he realized he probably had no other intrinsic skills than being a rock star. That's my answer. It's all I've ever done. It was kind of given, maybe from my perspective, not my dad's perspective, it was given that I would go into this business, because my of granddad, my uncle.

At the time that I broke into the business, I had worked two or three years in high school here in the business. Never had anything to do with the baseball end of it. I was always in our football department. My final two years of college, I was working part time for UPS, making ends meet as a college student and working at night for UPS. I was loading trucks, pushing trucks, whatever. When I graduated in 1982, I'm making $11.15 an hour. That's 30 years ago. Part time worker making $11.15 an hour.

My dad said, "Would they let you work full time?" "Yeah." The manager of the center I worked for had already told me, he says, "When you graduate, you got a job. You're going as a driver, but there's opportunity." To this day, a kid that I worked with probably knocks down about $300,000 a year as a middle manager at UPS. He's been working for them for 30 years. He does very well for himself. I told my dad, I said, "Yeah. They'll give me a job. I want to go work in the factory."

He made me pay for it, because when I graduated college and quit my job at UPS, he took me on working in the factory. He gave me an office job, and I was working in the factory too. $5.00 an hour, as a college graduate. $5.00 an hour. I made that for four years. So, why do I do it? Stupidity.

DJ: *Then I have to ask, what do you love about it?*

RS: Well, I love working in the factory. I love working in the small-town factory. I tell people that when I wake up in the morning—we get all the Dallas affiliates on our TV stations and stuff. I can wake up and lay in my bed, like I did this morning. They'll come on and they'll give a traffic report, and I'll just lay there and smile. They're talking about, "you got a 45-minute backup from the 930 highway blah, blah." I can get in my pickup and be here in four minutes.

I used to tell people when I lived in town. I said, "I can drive to work in three minutes. If I ride my bike, it's four minutes." Small town. The fact that I can work and do something that I like to do. I love working with the people out here, and I can do it in a small town. That's probably not as romantic as saying that I love the baseball business. Do I go to a lot of baseball games? No. We had Rangers tickets for years, and we would get to them as much as we could. I love going to games, but it was an hour and a half drive to the Rangers games. Do I follow baseball? Yeah, when the Rangers are doing well, I did. They had a great year this year. They passed out in the very end. I love the fact that it's a family business, so to speak. We've done it for years. It's all I know how to do.

. . . We're the only company in the world that will take their own product, being a ball glove, and repair it. There's eighty different brands of ball gloves in the world and we're the only one of those eighty that if something's wrong with it, you send it back to us and we can fix it for you. I'll say it's very import-ant—usually to men—that they keep that glove because grampa may have handed it down or dad or something like that. I say there's two things that men usually hold onto for most of their lives. That's their ball glove and their underwear. Going back to the premise of why you're here: It is Americana. It's our game.

Makers and Shapers—in Their Own Words—Part 2

For the most part, a manufactured glove bought in a store needs to be broken-in. Otherwise it will be too stiff to play with. The breaking-in of a ball glove is one of the signature rituals of the game of baseball and perhaps all of sports. The act of breaking-in a glove will put the user in to a world of contested prac-tices and beliefs passed down through generations and shared as wisdom by players (see Box 2.3 Practicing Anthropology: Break-In a Glove). Having a glove that fits the player's hand precisely is of no small importance, and it is perhaps not surprising that a cult of glove "masters," "doctors," "gurus" and "whisperers" has sprung up around the manufacture and breaking-in of gloves. These are the names in the baseball glove industry that take on a special aura, either for their designs or their work with specific players. Rawlings' Harry "Doc" Latina and his son, Rollie, "The Glove Doctor," certainly achieve this status, but so too does their successor Bob Clevenhagen, who has worked for Rawlings since 1977 (Fatsis, 2008). Perhaps the most famous cult figures in the glove world today are the

Breakout Box 2.2: Practicing Anthropology: Make a Glove

A glove is a commodity offered for sale. Professionally manufactured gloves are typically constructed of leather or in some cases synthetic fibers which therefore require access either to industrially tanned leather goods or bolts of specialized fabric. A manufactured glove requires access to capital, and to buy a glove produced professionally costs money. But that is not always the case; from the moment gloves were first introduced to the game, players have been devising their own gloves out of whatever materials are ready to hand. These do-it-yourself gloves are still a part of the game for many players who don't have access to the resources necessary for a commercially made glove. In a popular YouTube video former Yankees reliever Mariano Rivera describes how as a youth in Panama he would make a glove out of a cardboard box and demonstrates the technique for doing so. In another video Omar Vizquiel describes a similar glove he made as a boy. Players make gloves out of a variety of materials, including cardboard, newspaper, duct tape, and plastic milk jugs.

Cultural anthropologists who study material objects are interested in these individualized productions of material objects that circumvent the usual process of production and consumption. These practices are generally known as "hacks." As the cultural theorist McKenzie Wark explains in *A Hacker Manifesto* a hack "produces a production of a new kind, which has as its result a singular and unique product, and a singular and unique producer" (Wark, 2017). The origins of the glove can essentially be understood as a hack with early players cutting the fingers off of existing buckskin gloves or sewing the fingers together and stuffing them with padding to cushion the hand from harm. Ultimately, figures like Spalding and Irwin transformed those on-the fly innovations into marketable commodities produced for sale. According to Wark, this is precisely the life cycle of the hack:

> Production takes place on the basis of a prior hack which gives to production its formal, social, repeatable and reproducible form. Every production is a hack formalised and repeated on the basis of its representation. To produce is to repeat; to hack, to differentiate.

> (Wark, 2017)

Some cultural anthropologists have recently turned their attention to how such innovative hacking cultures embody the ethos and ethic of remaking and reshaping material and intellectual property outside of the typical patterns of production and consumption. A hack solves a problem, whether it be of scarcity of resources, deficiency of design, or legal and commercial impediments by virtue of ingenious workarounds. We can see these hacks as a preoccupation of a variety of cultures both past and present. "Hacking may be contemporary," the anthropologist Gabriella Coleman writes, "but the logic of its labor goes back centuries for it is a prime example of a 'craft'" (Coleman, 2010) For writers like Coleman and Wark, there is something democratic—although not unproblematically so—about hackers, "their hyper-elevation of meritocracy and individualism, both of which have a long and complicated life in the liberal tradition" (Coleman, 2010).

For theorists of hacking and anthropologists, coextensive with the celebration of creating something outside of the regular framework of industrial production there is a concern about judgment inherent in referring to these hacks as making-do and relegating the remade object to a second-class status. Finally, anthropologists of hacking understand that—perhaps in an even more intensive way than with ordinary commodities—the hack marks the hacker, either bodily or spiritually, as a different type of person. Coleman sees the hacker, in adopting that identity also adopting a political subjectivity and striking a blow for equality. "The hacker implementation of meritocracy–however imperfect and entwined with other modes of governance–seeks to constantly equalize the conditions for self-cultivation" (Coleman, 2008: 270). Wark, for his part, claims that the hack literally remakes the hacker. "Every hacker is at one and the same time producer and product of the hack, and emerges in its singularity as the memory of the hack as process" (Wark, 2017). This is certainly the case for the ballplayers who make their own gloves. Faced with an unforgiving piece of cardboard, fielders like Vizquiel, Rivera, Elvis Andrus and others had to develop the "soft hands" and quick exchange necessary to fielding at a high level.

As an exercise in hacking and to think through the design evolution of the glove students can hack their own gloves using everyday materials (see Figure 2.8). As you design and construct your glove consider what materials you'll be using. What features do you think are the most important? Flexibility? Strength? Padding? In what ways does your hacked glove solve a problem, improve on current design, or address a deficiency in gloves? Take your glove out for a catch. How successful is your hack? What do you observe about others' efforts? How does it change the way you catch a ball to be using a glove you made? What strengths and weaknesses are there to your design once it is put into practice?

Figure 2.8 **A homemade glove.** (*Source*: Photo by David Jenemann.)

Suggested Resources

Coleman, Gabriella E. "The Anthropology of Hackers," *The Atlantic*, September 21, 2010.

Coleman, Gabriella E. "Hacker Practice: Moral Genres and the Cultural Articulation of Liberalism." *Anthropological Theory* 8, no. 3 (2008): 255–277 www.theatlantic.com/technology/archive/2010/09/the-anthropology-of-hackers/63308/.

Wark, McKenzie. "A Hacker Manifesto [version 4.0]." 2017. www.subsol.c3.hu/subsol_2/contributors0/warktext.html.

Videos

www.youtube.com/watch?v=DwPM9x7GC9o.
www.lavidabaseball.com/stories-hof-cardboard-gloves/.

Japanese Glove designers Nobuyoshi Tsubota, longtime designer for Mizuno (see the "Signpost" below) and Shigeaki Aso, Wilson's "Glove Guru." Aso has become famous in recent years for a series of videos in which, sitting cross-legged on a mat, he demonstrates how to properly break-in a glove by dunking it in water and pounding it with a specialized mallet with the precise gestures of a martial artist or a samurai from a Kurosawa film (Breaking in a Glove with Aso, 2015). There is something mystical about these men's connection to the glove and their dedication to their craft. Ichiro Suzuki, the first Japanese superstar in the MLB speaks with eloquent reverence about the almost psychic connection he shares with Tsubota, who made nearly every glove the rightfielder has worn in his career:

> The Master can only listen with his ears to my demands about my glove. It's not like I make a sample that helps explain to him what I want. The ability to craft a tangible, high-precision object solely based on the information he hears is the definition of a master. Ordinary people can't do that. The feeling that I'm trying to capture when I put on a glove is different than another player's he might be making a glove for. So it's this uncanny ability to so precisely craft an object from an image that exists only in my mind that makes him a true virtuoso.

> (Lefton, 2008)

Perhaps not surprisingly in a consumer economy that produces nearly five million baseball gloves per year, in addition to these mythical glove designers, there has also arisen a group of professionals who specialize in breaking in gloves for customers so that they feel exactly right for the player (See Breakout Box 2.3). Dave Katz is one of these figures. He charges people who buy a glove from him $60 and people who send or bring him a glove $85 to break in their gloves, and I traveled to Meriden, CT to visit him and talk about the work of someone who does what he does for a living.

I must admit, I had an ulterior motive: When I first started playing baseball again about six years ago, I picked up an Easton glove from a sporting goods store that was going out of business. It was, at the time, one of Easton's nicer models, and even though it was heavily discounted, at $130, it was the most expensive glove I had ever bought. My buyer's remorse at spending so much on a glove was only amplified because the glove started out stiff and uncomfortable and proceeded to get worse each time I wore it. It never formed a proper pocket, and as a result was inadvertently responsible for the most spectacular play I had ever made. With a runner on first, I dove for a hard-hit ball deep up the middle at second base. The ball hit the pocket of my Easton and *exploded*—out of my glove, back to the bag and into the hands of our shortstop, who stepped on second and threw the ball to first, completing the double play. I'm sure it looked really cool, but there is no way I would have made either out, even if I had fielded the ball cleanly, and the only reason it happened is because I had never broken this Easton in properly.

If anyone could help me, The Glovesmith could. So, armed with my tape recorder, my camera, and my Easton, I drove to Meriden, about 45 minutes from Hartford to talk about baseball gloves and see if anything could be done for my stiff hunk of leather. Dave Katz's store is a small operation (see Figure 2.9). Along the walls and the center aisle of the store sit thigh-high shelves lined with baseball gloves—almost entirely Rawlings models. The royal blues, rich reds, and deep browns all side by side are—for someone who admires baseball gloves—truly beautiful. Within minutes of entering the store, Dave let me know that my Easton wasn't his favorite glove, and that I was wearing it all wrong. Instead of trying to fit my fingers into every stall, I should try putting my index and middle finger in ring-finger slot and the ring and pinky fingers in the last hole. Then, he told me, instead of trying to clasp the ball with all of my fingers,

> you should only squeeze from the last two and your thumb. It's like a peace sign. It's from there to there. These [index and middle] fingers you don't use. You make like you don't even have them. Here. Just for the heck of it, try it.

I took a ball, threw it at the glove and tried it. Suddenly, the ball was no longer popping out of the glove but getting enveloped in the pocket that formed in the place where my middle two fingers had been. I've worn a baseball glove for more than 40 years, and in 40 seconds, Dave Katz had changed my life. But what about how stiff the Easton was?

> Yes. I can actually take that thing. There's a little thing that I can do to that that'll take me two minutes and it'll soften it up appreciably. In order for me to get this little crease out of the thing, I have to do the whole thing [his process]. It's going to take me a week. You don't need it.

And then, at various points throughout the conversation, Dave would steal off into a room at the back of his shop and do something to my glove. He wouldn't let me see what he did, and he wouldn't tell me either (he also didn't charge me, because he didn't do "the whole thing"). He warned me that the glove would come back substantially darker, and it certainly did—darker, oily, and smelling of petroleum, but the glove was softer than it has ever been, and when we went outside to play catch, the ball went right into the pocket, every time. Here, indeed was a master.

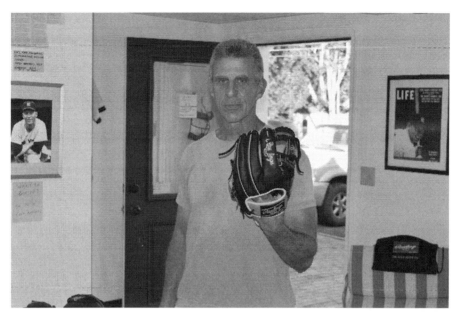

Figure 2.9 **"Glovesmith" Dave Katz (2017), Meriden, CT.** (*Source*: Photo by David Jenemann.)

DAVID JENEMANN: *How did you become a glovesmith?*

DAVE KATZ: I just dumbed into it. When I first got in the business, I decided just to, for the heck of it, throw a few gloves on the wall that I broke in, the way I had always done my gloves. Before you know it, it just caught on. Everybody that would come to me now, back then, would want one that I had already broken in.

    At first, I thought that people might think they were used, so it might be a turnoff. It ended up being just known in the area here, and people were just starting to come to me. It was just an experiment on my part, really. It just happened to work out. That was going back probably close to 40 years ago.

DJ: *When did you start specializing only in gloves?*

DK: I don't really remember when that happened. Maybe 25 years ago I decided, because I used to sell more varied sporting goods. Probably 25 years ago I just dumped everything and decided to do what I do best. Most of my sales were coming from the gloves. At that point, maybe that might have been a point where I decided this is where I'm going to make my money.

DJ: *I saw on your website that you also make gloves. Is that true?*

DK: I did. I never actually assembled them myself. I contracted people overseas to do them. I had a really nice following for those gloves, but when you're dealing with a situation where you can't actually be there to monitor what's going on, it's tough. You'll get some good stuff, you'll get some subpar stuff. Towards the end there, I started getting more subpar stuff than I was comfortable with. I've always sold Rawlings also. I was already a pretty big

Rawlings dealer. I just decided to forego the gloves unless I could find some-one to make them the way they needed to be made. If they're made the way I want them to be made, there's no better glove.

It's got to be a certain leather. When I talk to these people overseas, I have them send me gloves. I have them send me samples. I tell them the types of leathers that I want, this and that. They'll give me choices of what they supply. They need to send them to me and I need to break them in first. A lot of stuff looks great when you just look at it, but they all don't break in well. It has to be a glove that I can work with that can break in the way I want it to. If not, I just won't use those people. When you're dealing [overseas], everybody and their brother claims they make baseball gloves. They all claim they make the best. It's tough to find people that make really quality stuff. A lot of times they'll start you off with the really good stuff. Next order you get, this leather just doesn't feel the same as it did before.

. . . You don't remember back with the kangaroo gloves?

DJ: *Yes, I do, as a matter of fact. MacGregor did them [in the 1960s] and then Nokona does a kangaroo glove too [the Buckaroo™ now mainly for softball players].*

DK: Yes, Nokona, but it wasn't like the MacGregor ones. The MacGregor ones, every single one of my buddies had one. I had one, my brother had . . . this was after we bought those $3 ones at Barker's Department Store. We got more expensive ones later. Every single one turned into tissue paper right here [at a place on the palm near the hinge] where you could just pull it up. Every guy's glove ripped right there. It's all that thin.

DJ: *Why do you only sell Rawlings?*

DK: I can sell whatever I want, but they [sporting goods stores] are all doing it. When I decided just to do Rawlings, the companies really weren't doing that yet. I decided probably 15 years ago on just doing Rawlings just because they're the nicest glove by far. I just wanted to pick one rather than trying to make everybody happy, buy some of this, some of that. If I was going to pick one, I decided it was Rawlings.

There comes a point where if it's not the way I want it to be, I'm just not going to do it. The last couple of years, I've been looking for people to do them the way I want them, and it's just not happening. I'm perfectly happy with the Rawlings stuff that I have. I haven't missed a beat as far as sales. If anything, they've increased.

DJ: *Who is your primary customer?*

DK: Maybe six or seven-years-old to maybe 16-years-old. First real glove they've gotten. College kids, you don't get that many. To be honest with you, by the time that six-year-old is college age, 90 percent of them aren't playing any-more. It's very few kids that actually get to college from tee ball, very, very few. Even high school, a lot of them are sorted out. It's that age where the parents are still really psyched about the kid, and they've got all sorts of dreams in their head for him or her. I sell as many gloves to girls as I do to boys. Girls' fast pitch is huge.

This is where you're spending money for your kids for their sports and everything. You're trying to get them the nicest stuff you can and give them all the advantages you can. By the time they hit high school or whatever, a lot of them aren't even playing that sport anymore. They're on to something else, and college for sure you don't find many. When I was a kid, you couldn't start Little League until you were eight. These kids now are starting tee ball at four and five. People are upgrading their equipment. By the time they're eight, they all want to buy them $300 gloves. It's ridiculous.

DJ: *But it keeps you in business, I imagine.*

DK: I'm not going to lie. I make more money now than I ever did just because of all the crazy travel parents that need to get their kid the best possible . . . the most expensive, not the most advantageous. You can find an 11 and a quarter inch glove that's small, but it's constructed for a Jose Altuve. Everything has got to be age appropriate. You're not buying your kid's sneakers now that they're going to have in high school. You have to buy them age appropriate stuff. The little lightweight $40 gloves are where an eight-year-old kid should be. I deal with a whole segment of people that want expensive because they have the thing, if I buy them something that's 300 bucks, it's going to help them, but it's going to hurt them tremendously, not helping at all. That's a large part of my clientele. I can talk some of them off the cliff, but not a lot of them.

DJ: *They clearly haven't seen the video that Mariano Rivera does of making a glove out of the cardboard box, which is what he did growing up as a kid.*

DK: I always get them with this. I'll ask them, "Did your father ever want to run and buy you [this glove]? Would he have ever bought you a $200 glove or a $300 glove," and it's always no. I'll say, "He just threw you a glove, and you loved it, and you used it forever. You didn't say, 'Geez, Dad, I need one for second base. Now I'm playing right field and I need one for right field.' You didn't complain about the color. You just used it and you loved it. You probably never even knew what size it was." Actually, back then, they didn't put sizes in gloves, so you wouldn't have known. Today, with the internet and all the travel stuff, and everybody's a little expert, there's way too much info out there. You'd be stunned how many people stress over that, over little things. It's no more difficult than it was when your father gave you your first glove. People make it more difficult.

DJ: *Do you remember any of them you played with when you were younger?*

DK: I remember walking into a local department store, way back before there were any department stores per se. They had some MacGregor gloves in there for $2.99. We bought a two-field . . . My brother and myself were with my father. We were just kids. We each bought a glove. We bought, I think, a first baseman's mitt or maybe a catcher's mitt along with it. Those are really the only ones as a kid that I remember, those MacGregor gloves. I actually think that maybe our first gloves came from the local little hardware/everything store. It was called Liberty Stores. I think, because at that time, people like that, you could buy a hammer in there or you could buy a baseball glove or electric trains. I remember getting Lionel trains in there. I'm pretty sure we got gloves from there, but I don't remember what they were.

DJ: *How do your customers find you?*

DK: The way it works is you'll go tell somebody, show them this glove that you've had for 10 years and that you never liked, and he or she might call me. My whole thing now is word of mouth other than the internet has helped tremendously, but it works the same way there. If I sell a glove to someone in Idaho, they'll tell you and you'll call me. It works that way. It's a spider web thing. It takes longer because I don't really go out and promote myself. I don't really push. The long-term effect is, when you get a loyal customer, when I get one, they pretty much stick with me.

DJ: *So what is it about the baseball glove?*

DK: I deal with a lot of guys that are glove nuts. There was a detective out in New Haven who used to bring me a glove every few months to break in. His kids weren't playing anymore. I would say, "What are you doing with these things because your sons aren't playing anymore?" He admitted to me one day that his wife threatened to divorce him if he didn't stop buying these things. He would bring me all these oddball gloves that you've never even heard of.

He bought a catcher's mitt from me. I said, "What are you doing with this? Your kid doesn't catch anymore and you're not playing." He goes, "I'll sit on a stakeout tonight. I'll just sit there and I'll go like this [pounds his baseball glove]." There are certain people that just have a glove thing. They like to feel a glove on your hand. You can understand. You can understand that. I've got customers in certain places . . . one guy in California, he must have sent me two dozen gloves already over the last seven or eight years. He'll give me a different story each time; he's helping kids out in the neighborhood, he's doing this, he's doing that. I really think it's that the guy just loves gloves. It's hard to explain, but I'll find myself with a glove on my hand, just walking over and grabbing one and putting it on my hand. When my friends come in, to a guy, they almost all do it. They'll all go grab a glove and sit there and talk to me with a glove in their hand . . . You just like the way the thing feels on your hand. It's weird. My brother will walk in. He'll grab a glove and put it on his hand. I just like the way that thing feels on there.

Breakout Box 2.3: Practicing Anthropology: Breaking-in a Glove

Of all of the things ever written and said about breaking in a baseball glove, the poet Christopher Buckley might put it best: "Breaking in a new glove involved myth, ritual, and resources, and sorting through all three."

(Buckley, 2008: 89)

Buckley proceeds to catalogue all of the ways a player in the middle part of the twentieth century could accomplish the task.

As more modern mitts were made, from the 1940s through the '60s, they truly had to be broken in, as the cowhide and thicker steerhide made a new mitt very stiff. Glove companies developed and sold many different conditioners to soften up new leather and to keep leather pliable. Lexol was one, and another was Nokona Classic Glove Conditioner, which came in a tube with the company's classic emblem of an American Indian on it. In the late '50s A.G. Spalding offered Speed-EE Baseball Glove or Mitt Dressing Oil in a red can with a plastic spout. From the late 1940s and '50s, Double Play Glove Conditioner contained mink oil and came in a five-inch-tall can. During those years Rawlings promoted Glovolium Baseball Glove Dressing, in a tin about the size cigarette lighter fluid came in, and Sears sold a two-ounce tube of Glove Conditioner—"especially for the care of fine baseball gloves." Neat's-foot oil (rendered from the feet and shinbones of cattle) was the one we all knew about, but no one had the money to buy and compare glove conditioning oils. Someone said rubbing bacon grease into the pocket, then baking the glove in the oven at 150-degree heat was the way to go, but I never saw that done. And a kid or two used Vaseline, which some glove repair specialists use even today. Mostly, we broke in our gloves playing a lot of catch, using them, stiff or not, in game after game, and repeatedly throwing a ball into the pocket from about a foot away and gloving it as we sat around talking—almost a nervous habit while watching a game or waiting for one to start.

(Buckley, 2008: 89–90)

From the earliest days of the discipline, cultural anthropologists have been interested in the practices and prohibitions of cultural rituals (Lévi-Strauss,

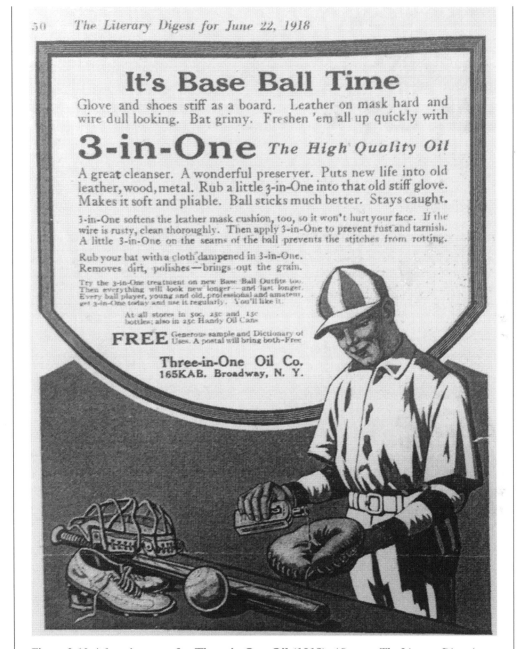

Figure 2.10 **Advertisement for Three-in-One Oil (1918).** (*Source*: *The Literary Digest.*)

Boas). One of the key tools of anthropological observation is an understanding of how those cultural rituals are promulgated and passed on. Like almost no other object in contemporary sport, a baseball glove demands modification—breaking-in—and that breaking-in process is a highly contested ritual of the game practiced by nearly everyone who plays (unless, of course they have the resources to enlist the expertise of a "glove doctor"). A simple ethnographic exercise is to ask a dozen people how to break in a glove, and you will likely get a dozen answers about how to accomplish a task that has happened millions of times each year for more than a century (see Figure 2.10).

Consider just a few of the variations on the ritual that you can find by searching on Google, interviewing informants, visiting a sporting goods store, or observing a fellow player:

"Steam it."
"Dunk it in water."
"Pound it with a mallet."
"Tie two baseballs in the pocket and put it under your mattress."
"Put it in a warm oven."
"Put it in a microwave oven for thirty seconds."
"Put it in the dryer."
"Run a car wheel over it."
"Rub it with glove oil."
"Rub it with shaving cream."
"Rub it with Vaseline."
"Just play catch with it."

Each of these suggestions comes with their own variations and sub-questions. Perhaps the most idiosyncratic version I heard from my fellow VTMSBL players was this one:

> I most recently put my newly bought glove in the dishwasher, sans dishes, so as not to muck up one of my more valuable possessions— both in terms of sentimentality and price. Following, I turned the glove inside and out several times, and the placed a softball in the pocket, added a rubber band or two, and let it dry. I may have slept on it for a day or two as well.

> (VTMSBL player)

But what temperature should the water be? What temperature should my oven be? Under my mattress or under my pillow? What type of oil or shaving cream should I use? Depending on the site, informant, or participant, their own agendas and their own set of beliefs, for every practice someone insists on following, you will likely also hear a bevy of prohibitions:

"Don't get it wet; it will cause the leather to crack."
"Don't put it in the oven; it will dry out the leather and make the laces brittle."

"Don't use oil; it will make the glove heavy."
"Don't do anything; just play catch with it."

For an assignment, if your class has a budget, purchase a few gloves. Have students research some methods for breaking in a glove. There are a number of websites and YouTube videos that will demonstrate how to do it. Some of the most popular feature Wilson's "Glove Guru" Shigeaki Aso (www.youtube.com/watch?v=3i_x0neoseU). Another comes from the website The Art of Manliness (www.artofmanliness.com/2009/04/19/how-to-break-in-a-baseball-glove/). Pay attention to the comment sections of these videos. What do they tell you about the various techniques and practices? As you manipulate the glove, what works best? When is the glove broken-in? The anthropologist Tim Ingold, writes of teaching his students to weave baskets:

> We laboured for almost three hours, gradually developing a rhythm and a feel for the material. As the work progressed, however, we began to face another problem. How would we know when to stop?. . . The end dawned for us, not when the form came to match initial expectations, for we had none.

> (Ingold, 2013: 23)

For Ingold's students, they knew when they were done when they were done. There is something of the same reality in breaking in a glove. Imperceptibly, through repetition, and pounding, and massaging, and trial and error, *a* glove will somehow transform into *your* glove. And then you'll know.

Suggested Reading

Ingold, T. *Making: Anthropology, Archaeology, Art and Architecture.* Taylor & Francis, 2013.

Signposts: Endorsements

The first glove I remember—one that still lives in my parent's garage, waiting for one more game of catch—was a Sears & Roebuck Ted Williams model. I don't remember how I got the glove—or even if it was originally mine—but I remember wondering, as a kid growing up in the 1970s, who Ted Williams was. The Rawlings Reggie Jackson model that eventually replaced the Sears Ted Williams glove seemed a lot less anachronistic. Every kid playing baseball in those days knew who Reggie was. The fact that, as a now-ardent Red Sox fan, I cherished a Reggie Jackson glove much more than a Ted Williams model is no small irony to me. However, be it "Teddy Ballgame" or "The Straw that Stirs the Drink," it certainly never struck me as strange that a glove would bear the signature of a current or former player. Gloves took on their personality, their abilities, and their "cool" by virtue of whose signature was on them. Reggie was cool. You could see him playing on TV. Ted Williams was some old guy who didn't even play the game anymore.

Just as the glove comes relatively late to the game, the idea of endorsing a glove is a comparatively recent innovation. Strictly speaking, of course, the first gloves advertised for sale in the nineteenth century were endorsed gloves, bearing the names of Albert Spalding or Arthur Irwin, both former players, but paying players to endorse gloves was generally introduced in the twentieth century, notably in the 1920s, when players like Babe Ruth, Lou Gehrig, and Ty Cobb all agreed to have their names on gloves. Some would agree to the endorsement for a fee or royalties on gloves sold; others would endorse a glove in exchange for free gloves from the manufacturers. In a handwritten 1924 letter to the Draper & Maynard Company, Washington Senator pitcher Walter Johnson writes: "Dear Sirs, Would you make me a G40 glove? I like it better than my own model. Please send it to Washington D.C. c/o Ball Club. Thanking you for past favors and don't hesitate if I can do anything for you in regards to the gloves or anything else" (National Baseball Hall of Fame and Museum. Clippings File "Baseball Gloves"). Draper & Maynard took Johnson up on his offer, reproducing a facsimile of the letter in an otherwise imageless advertisement framed by the words: "AN UNSOLICITED LETTER GIVEN US WHOLLY ON MERIT PROVING OUR CLAIM THAT THE BIG LEAGUE PLAYERS USE D. & M. GOODS" (National Baseball Hall of Fame and Museum. Clippings File "Baseball Gloves").

The two most significant of these early endorsements, from the standpoint of the development of the practice were the 1920 "Lucky Dog" glove (see Figure 2.11) endorsed by Babe Ruth for Draper & Maynard—the same company that sold Arthur "Foxy" Irwin's first glove—and the Ken-Wel zipper-back first baseman's mitt endorsed by Lou Gehrig. Although neither glove manufacturer is still in business today, these endorsements were noteworthy, both because they involved popular players from the most successful team of the 1920s, the New York Yankees (although Ruth's relationship with Draper & Maynard dated to his days with the Red Sox), and because in today's collectors market, signature model versions of the Gehrig and Ruth gloves are among the most valuable gloves on the market, each selling recently for over $10,000 (Seideman, 2014, 2017).

Sporting goods manufacturers vary in their use of endorsed equipment. Some opted for a less is more approach. In 1962, Sears signed Ted Williams not

Figure 2.11 **"Lucky Dog" advertisement featuring Babe Ruth (1920).** (*Source*: Plymouth State University Digital Collections.)

only to endorse their gloves, but to oversee their "Ted Williams Sports Advisory Staff" in charge of quality control for all of their sporting and outdoor equipment. A press release posted as an article about the Sears deal appearing in *Sports Illustrated* asked "Why did Sears sign Ted Williams?"

> For one simple reason. To add a cold, professional viewpoint on the quality of every piece of Sears sports equipment before it gets into the Sears catalog or any one of the 740 Sears department stores . . . He personally field-tests them. And he suggests improvements in order to keep Sears a stride ahead in the sporting goods field. He may recommend putting bigger, stronger wheels on a camp trailer. Lighter soles on a pair of hunting boots. Softer leather in the liner of a fielder's glove—to create the proper "feel." . . . And that's the reason for signing Ted Williams. If the legendary Williams batting eye can't detect a flaw, Sears knows the item is absolutely first-rate.

("Why did Sears sign Ted Williams?" 1962)

As Ben Bradlee recounts in his biography of Williams, the deal Sears inked with Williams was for five years at $125,000 a year, but that was just a base figure; Williams also got a percentage of anything sold with his name on it. Sears would seem to have gotten their money's worth. Bradlee reports Williams actively vetted everything from fishing rods to camping gear in addition to his signature baseball gloves (Bradlee, 2013).

Some companies took a "more is more" approach. In a Rawlings Press Release from January 5, 1964, the company touted their "Big 8" Glove:

> Baseball Gloves have been endorsed by leading players for many years, but Rawlings' new glove—the Big 8—is endorsed by <u>eight</u> of the top major league stars. The Big 8 are Ken Boyer, Tommy Davis, Dick Groat, Mickey Mantle, Brooks Robinson, Warren Spahn, Tom Tresh, and Billy Williams.
>
> (National Baseball Hall of Fame and Museum.
> Clippings File "Baseball Gloves")

What's noteworthy about the "Big 8" is that in addition to the fact that there are eight endorsers and eight key design elements of the glove, the group endorsing the glove is a multi-racial mix with six white players (Boyer, Groat, Mantle, Robinson, Spahn, and Tresh) and two African Americans (Davis and Williams).

And some companies take a minimalist approach to endorsements. Although Hall of Famer Nolan Ryan currently touts the merits of Nokona gloves, and in the past the Nokona company has had signature models, today, Nokona eschews signing players to endorsement contracts, preferring to emphasize the quality of their mitts and their made-in-America ethos to convince younger players to use their gloves over paying for endorsements:

> When I say we never will, we never will because currently the market is just not there . . . We can't throw money into these people. We try to have our own farm system, so to speak. We don't go out and try to get the big-name players. We talk to these young kids and tell them the Nokona story. We're not going to make you rich, but we're going to help your game, and we're going to help you be an MLB player.
>
> (Rob Storey interview)

Mizuno's Foray Into the United States

One of the most significant developments in the history of the glove has been the movement of glove manufacturing to other countries. "In 1990," Jonathan Light claims, "Rawlings and Nokona were the only two companies making gloves in the United States. Other sources reported that by 1993 there were almost no Major Leaguers using American-Made gloves" (Light, 2005: 352). Today, Nokona is the only significant baseball glove manufacturer still operating entirely within the United States (Mayeda, 2017). Rawlings, Wilson, Spalding, and the other longstanding manufacturers of this key piece of equipment for the "national pastime" have moved their production almost entirely offshore, with the exception of a few high-end custom models. Even Nokona is feeling the effects of globalization. Despite marketing themselves as the lone hold-out against outsourcing, a closer look at their glove tags reveals that they are "90% Domestic Materials; 100% USA labor," reflecting the fact that they are sourcing some of their material including leather from other countries (Nokona.com, Gwynne, 2007).

For the most part, however, a glove worn today is likely to be produced in China, the Philippines, or in Mexico, even if the leather is sourced in the United States. This globalization has a long history. Indeed, given that Arthur Irwin was a Canadian, it could be argued that the manufacturing of baseball gloves has always had an international component. Nevertheless, following Latour's logic that material objects always involve a process of "circulations, sequences, transfers, translations, displacements, [and] crystallisations," it is worth considering Mizuno's 1970s foray into America as one of the key signposts on the way to a general acceptance of foreign-made gloves.

In 1978, US and Japanese representatives of the Mizuno company outfitted a trailer with leather and glove-making equipment and drove around Florida to Major League spring training facilities making gloves for prospects and established players. "Ballplayers who visit the van are measured on the spot and a glove is made for them within hours instead of weeks as with other firms" (Werzer, 1979).

Mizuno, at the time the largest sporting goods manufacturer in Japan, had produced gloves for Wilson, Rawlings and other companies for a number of years, but the glove trailer road trip represented their first effort to capture the US market directly.

Initially, what began as a grass roots effort targeted at a handful of players would blossom into a substantial presence for Mizuno in the US marketplace. One of the early converts to Mizuno gloves was Bobby Valentine, who would ultimately manage teams in Japan and develop a friendship with Mizuno's legendary designer Nobuyoshi Tsubota who had traveled with the Mizuno van. Bob Boone and Dusty Baker were also early wearers, and Bill "Spaceman" Lee told me that he thought he was one of the first American professionals to wear Mizuno gloves. Valentine remembered later that many players still maintained their contracts with American companies while secretly wearing their Mizuno gloves, sometimes obscuring or removing the labels. Mizuno officials promoted this practice, preferring to have players wear their gloves and tell other players by word of mouth. "We tell them when they come into the van that we don't want to do anything that would jeopardize their contract with someone else," claimed Jim Darby, the US Mizuno representative on the van tour. "Even though they're under contract to someone else, they keep coming back to us" (Moore, 1981). The one exception to the word of mouth campaign was Pete Rose, who reportedly received $100,000 per year personal appearances contract, at the time a sizable figure. "I'd rather not say how much we pay him, but it's a lot of money," said Ken Kondo, an executive vice president with Mizuno. "It's worth it though, he's very good at it" (Moore, 1981). The strategy proved successful: in the three years following the first foray of the Mizuno van, Mizuno estimated that 150 players were wearing their gloves—nearly 20 percent of Major League Baseball. Needless to say, Rawlings and Wilson denied how successful Mizuno's inroads were, "We're concerned about them, but I don't think they've had much impact." But whatever the actual success of the road trip, the lasting legacy of Mizuno's mobile van is that it revealed that glove manufacturing was now a global enterprise and no longer an America-only industry. Not only did Mizuno's custom-made strategy help the Japanese company gain a foothold in the United States, it shone a light on the fact that many "American" glove manufacturers had already moved their operations overseas.[2]

Notes

1 This exception is challenged by the Insignia company making gloves in a factory in Worcester Massachusetts. However, their relationship to Nokona is a complex one, as at one point Nokona and Insignia were owned by the same investment company, and Insignia still uses many of Nokona's designs.
2 Flash forward to 2017 and it is worth noting that Nokona, the last predominately US glove manufacturer is sending vans to high schools and colleges to make custom gloves for players.

3

MEANING

My most memorable glove was a Wilson A2000 infielder's glove that I broke
in to perfection with all the fingers curving inwards at their ends to reliably
envelop arriving grounders. I got the glove in high school and used it to
play second base in my junior and part of my senior year (before our
catcher broke his thumb and I moved behind the plate). The glove's finest
hour came in the Vermont State Division II championship game when it
fielded a hard ground-hugging ball to end the game with the tying run on
third and the winning run also on base. Somewhere along the way, in my
30s I believe, the glove disappeared. I still can remember its gratifying,
heavy feel and I miss it. It was one of the most satisfying belongings I have
ever owned.

(VTMSBL player)

Having considered aspects of the historical and material evolution of the
baseball glove, we can now turn our attention to the question of meaning.
"Meaning" is a thorny topic. Objects in the world exist for certain purposes and
figure in specific cultural practices. Nevertheless, the mode of their existence
and the way they are used gives them what we conventionally call their meaning.
The meanings of objects, ideas, and events are often contested based on the
individual background and context of who is using them and interpreting them.
Even where "truth conditions are identical," the Nobel-prize winning behavioral economist Daniel Kahneman reminds us, the interpretation of even two
"logically equivalent statements," can depend "entirely on what you mean by
meaning" (Kahneman, 2011: 363). We have seen how a baseball glove has been
a site of contested meanings from its earliest introduction when beliefs about its
effeminizing power came into conflict with its practical utility. Depending on
who was—or wasn't—adopting the glove, the "truth" of the baseball glove's role
in the game has always been a matter of dispute.

Social scientists and cultural critics have a variety of ways of thinking about
the process of meaning-making that considers both our cultural practices

concerning objects and our interpretations of those practices. Often, the meaning of an object is—at first blush—eminently pragmatic. A baseball glove is what it is because of what it's used for and because it isn't anything else. As we have seen in the previous chapter, design plays a part in giving an object its pragmatic meaning. Let's think about how that works for a baseball glove: A baseball glove is still a glove, and originally, it was a glove like many others, a work glove or a driving glove, retooled to play a game, but over the course of its history, it has evolved to do one task extremely well—catching a baseball. However, in terms of helping us do most other glove-things, it's practically useless.

We wear gloves and mittens for many tasks. They keep our hands warm when it's cold, but they also protect our hands from heat when we grasp a hot pot-handle or a tray from the oven. I wear gloves in the garden or when splitting wood to protect my hands from thorns, stings, and blisters. My doctor and my dentist and their assistants wear silicone gloves when performing an examination or a procedure. Some people wear gloves when doing dishes or scuba-diving. Others wear opera gloves with a dress or a tuxedo. Historically, a glove could function as a token to a lover, and a slap with a glove could provoke a duel. In the context of the European monarchy, the glove historically functioned as a formal signifier of power, and Stallybrass and Jones remind us, "the monarch's glove continued to be treated as. . . an extension of the monarch's hand throughout the seventeenth century" (Stallybrass and Jones, 2001: 17–18).

Gloves are also of course, vital in the world of sports. Boxing would be an even more brutal and bloody affair without them. Golfers use them to grip a club; hockey players don gloves to hold their sticks and protect their knuckles. Baseball even has two different types of gloves, the ones for batting and the ones for fielding—the subject of this book.

As a result of its evolution, a baseball glove is useless for nearly all of these tasks, save the one—fielding, not least of the reasons for which being the fact that you only wear one of them. A baseball glove wouldn't keep your hands warm; it's extremely bad at gripping an axe handle; and I would run in the other direction from a doctor who tried to do a procedure on me who happened to be wearing one.

What it is good at doing, and this is very much a function of its design—is catching a baseball. The cliché is that form follows function; put it another way, material begets meaning. A baseball glove is meant to catch a baseball, and its design has evolved accordingly. Its production, its marketing, and its sale are tailored to address this purpose.

Since the glove is so specialized, one of the first constellation of meanings that adhere to the glove are those regarding its proper use in the field. Throughout the history of the game, coaches, players, and glove manufacturers have been exchanging tips, strategies, and wisdom for fielders on how to use the glove.

In Chad Harbach's novel, *The Art of Fielding*, one of the main characters, Henry Scrimshander, a shortstop prodigy at a small Midwest college, obsesses over the advice he reads in a guide to fielding written by the fictional St. Louis Cardinals shortstop Aparicio Rodriguez, Rodriguez, an amalgamation of Hall-of-Famers Luis Aparicio and Ozzie Smith, delivers zen-like advice on proper fielding techniques. "The glove is not an object in the usual sense" Rodriguez claims. "For the infielder to divide it from himself, even in thought, is one of the roots of error" (Harbach, 2011: 8). Although "*The Art of Fielding*," the book supposedly written by Rodriguez, is a fiction, it nevertheless echoes a long tradition of how-to manuals for proper glove-work dating back to the turn of the twentieth century. These range from Arthur Irwin's *Practical Ball Playing* (Irwin, 1895) to *Baseball for Dummies* by Hall of Fame 2nd baseman Joe Morgan (2014). The Spalding company, which was behind Irwin's book and was adept at wringing every possible dollar out of baseball, not surprisingly put out a series of these guides in the first decades of the 1900s specific to individual positions. Although most of these guides are prosaic, some sparkle with the same sort of poetry as does the one written by Harbach's fictional Cardinals shortstop. In Matteson's *How to Play the Outfield* (see Figure 3.1), for example, the author advises:

If you are a right-handed thrower your left hand is covered with a glove. It is a pretty big glove. The thing to do is to put up the gloved hand between the eyes and the sun. You can peep around the edge of the mitt and watch the ball until you are ready to catch it.

(Matteson, 1905: 17)

As with the image we looked at in the first of the book's "Practicing Anthropology" boxes, where a player wearing a glove was catching barehanded. There is something idiosyncratic about the cover of *How to Play the Outfield*: the outfielder is wearing a mitt more appropriate to a catcher or a first baseman rather than the glove an outfielder would wear. Here again we see evidence of a practice in transition before there is an accepted form that everyone recognizes.

Today, for the most part, the advice is more prosaic. YouTube videos take the place of printed how-to manuals. A Google search of "how to play the outfield" turns up 410,000 video results. Much of the information constitutes solid advice—although not much has fundamentally changed since 1905. But let the buyer beware, one of the top hits is by "Domingo Ayala" a parody series of how-to videos hosted by a fictional Dominican ballplayer "born and raised in Puerto Plata, DR sometime between 1978 and 1988" (domingobeisbol.com).

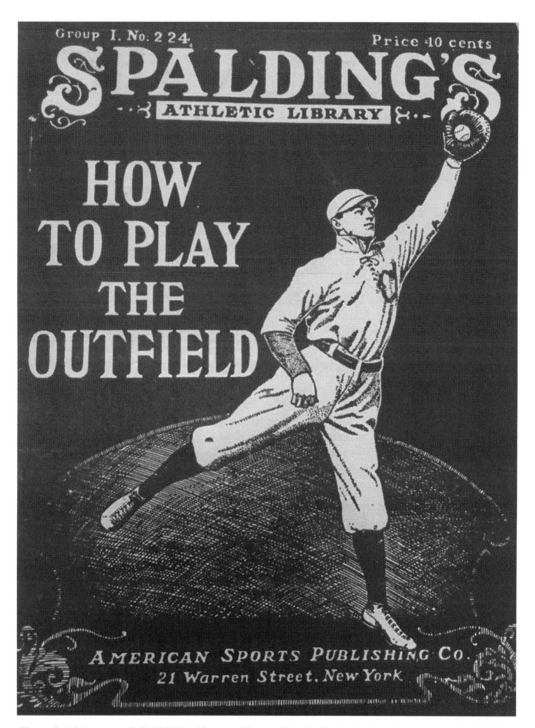

Figure 3.1 **Matteson, J. F. (1905).** (*Source*: *How to Play the Outfield*: American Sports Publishing Company.)

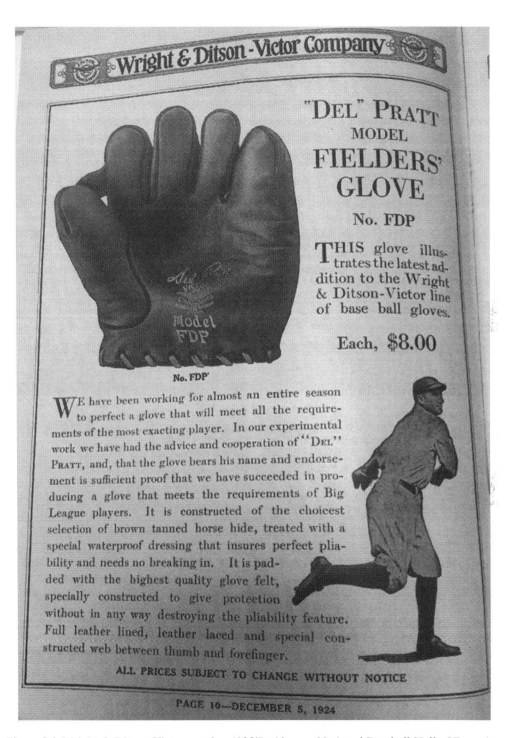

Figure 3.2 **Wright & Ditson-Victor catalog (1925).** (*Source*: National Baseball Hall of Fame.)

Another "official" discourse about the meaning of the glove comes from the manufacturers who utilize descriptions of their product designed to appeal to potential customers. These statements may not be rooted in reality and often attach certain qualities to the glove based on the historical tradition embodied by the company, the quality of the leather used in manufacture, notions of craftsmanship, or desirable qualities and design innovations purported to make ballplayers better or more adept at fielding. From the earliest days of the glove's first production and sale, this rhetoric has predominated. In a 1924 advertisement for a Del Pratt model of a Wright & Ditson-Victor fielder's glove, the manufacturers claim that they have been working for "almost an entire season" to produce a glove up to the task of being worn by a professional player (see Figure 3.2).

The "Del" Pratt model Wright & Ditson-Victor glove sold for $8.00 in 1925. Today, Rawlings markets its top of the line Gold Glove model and attempts to justify its $500 price by evoking the same rhetoric:

The culmination of 100 years of Rawlings' glove-making craftsmanship, the new Rawlings Gold Glove series with Opti-Core™ Technology delivers the ultimate in playability and feel, inspiring a new generation of defensive excellence. These gloves feature flawless, European leather famous for its supple feel and durable finish combined with special features like hand-sewn welting and ultra-premium, luxury palm lining comfortably completes a fit and feel that can only be described as custom. These gloves are meticulously cut, assembled and sewn, start to finish, by a single craftsman, all Rawlings Gold Gloves carry an individual serial number signifying the maker, the date created and the glove's production number.

(Rawlings Sporting Goods, n.d.)

For its part, Wilson markets its Custom A2K—a comparative bargain at $359—in a similar fashion:

The A2K®, Wilson's most premium series of baseball glove, is made with Pro Stock Select leather chosen for its consistency and flawlessness—the ideal leather for a glove. Glove Master Craftsman Shigeaki Aso designs all gloves in the A2K® line with Rolled Dual Welting ™ to provide long-lasting shape, Double Palm Construction for maximum pocket stability and extra shaping from our craftsmen so all A2K®s break in quicker and last longer.

(Wilson Sporting Goods, n.d.)

Furthermore, in addition to the glovemakers selling contemporary designs and evoking craftsmanship and tradition, there are a number of niche baseball equipment manufacturers trying to capture the nostalgia market by promoting "vintage" model gloves. A company called the Vintage Baseball Factory markets a "Foxy Irwin Glove" (vbbf.com), while Akadema, a company that also manufactures contemporary designs, also offers its "Hoboken Collection" of vintage gloves including "a remake of the 1929 Babe Ruth RFO Reach snap back mitt. Play like Babe or display it in your sports collection or office desk." The glove, Akadema claims, "comes with a letter of authenticity" (Akadema).

In the book *Branded*, author Jason Lee describes Akadema's "vintage" strategy:

Glove collectors who don't want to pay $1000 for the real item buy these gloves. Executives buy them to place their favorite autographed balls in . . . Akadema now owns trademarks of some of the oldest brand names, such as Reach (1880) and Ken-Wel (1916), which leads them to lightheartedly state that their brands are as old as some of their competitors.

(Lee, 2010: 17–18)

There is a lot to unpack in each of these descriptions and a lot of questions a discerning, anthropologically-minded customer might ask: What makes "European leather" more supple than leathers from other continents? What makes an item "most premium?" Isn't that a redundancy? Is "Rolled Dual Welting™" better than "hand-sewn welting?" What meanings do letters of authenticity or individualized serial numbers convey in the context of an industrially produced object? We will return to these descriptions at the end of the chapter when we consider one of the glove's meanings in terms of the concept of value, but in the case of both of these descriptions, the "meaning" of the glove rests in its purportedly exceptional qualities, qualities that many leather and glove experts will admit, are really just marketing strategies. As the glovesmith Dave Katz told me when I interviewed him:

It's all cowhide. If you just check the internet and look at all the different terminology there is, every single manufacturer throws out a bunch of marketing gibberish to entice you to buy. It's this kind of leather, that kind of leather. [Rawlings has] a Pro Preferred and they have what they call a Gold Glove, which is a $500 glove, [but] anything over a Heart of the Hide [approx. $200] is 100% marketing.

The discourses about how best to use the glove on the field and the commercial discourses about a glove's qualities coalesce around an aspirational marker of value specific to the game, the Rawlings Gold Glove Award, the annual award presented to Major League players for defensive performance. Rawlings instituted the Gold Glove Award in 1957, initially for the nine best defensive players in all of baseball (one for each position), but the following year, Rawlings and the coaches and managers who selected the recipients expanded the award to give Gold Gloves in both the National and American Leagues.

The award itself is a Rawlings baseball glove coated in gold lamé attached to a walnut board. Perhaps befitting an award designed to look like something more valuable than it is, the Gold Glove Award has long been controversial, often honoring the same players year after year when many other players with better fielding percentages, better range, or other qualities that might make them a better candidate for the award have been passed over. In an effort to avoid some of these oversights, in 2013, in addition to the votes by managers and coaches, Rawlings started weighting the candidates with a statistical measure called the SABR Defensive Index (SDI). However, as the statistical website fivethirtyeight.com argues, the SDI may have swung the pendulum completely away from the qualitative and subjective assessment of fielding and swayed the votes of the coaches who see the numbers. As SABR's president claims, "We think it's influenced the managers' and coaches' voting" (Paine and Bialik, 2015). Here as in many other aspects of the game, one of the distinctive cultural idiosyncrasies of baseball is the ongoing debate over value between proponents of quantitative and qualitative data. In keeping with the vexed and contradictory history and myths of the baseball glove, the value of a Gold Glove award is never simple.

Theories of Meaning

Another set of discourses that help give gloves their meaning is the body of theoretical analysis written by material culture scholars. Little or nothing has been written about baseball gloves from a theoretical perspective, but the ideas of cultural theorists can help us understand how a humble object of everyday use becomes meaningful. We have touched on a number of these theoretical ideas already, but it is worth considering some of the key figures in cultural anthropology who shed light more generally on how commonplace objects take on meaning in the world. Perhaps the cultural anthropologist whose career has provided the most sustained consideration of materiality is Daniel Miller. As we have seen, Miller considers material objects as parts of the social fabric of society that are both made by and remake individuals who come into contact with them. By virtue of their concreteness, and the fact that cultural practices using objects evolve over time, Miller argues that emphasizing the materiality of things helps us avoid the trap of thinking too abstractly and deterministically about notions of value and meaning. In order to confront objects honestly, we must meet them as they are, that is as concretely existing in the material world. "[I]n using the term 'material culture,'" he argues,

> we believe that there are many ways in which the results can be far less fetishistic than many of those works that do not purport to have such an object focus. At the same time the intention is to focus upon the artefactual world without being founded in any general theory of artefacts or material culture.

(Miller, 2002: 5)

In another of his works called *Materiality*, Miller refines the idea that material anthropology forces us to countenance the world as one of "unordered diversity." Anthropology, as a methodology and a habit of mind demands that the anthropologist never rest easily in their certainty about what "stuff" means from moment to moment:

> What anthropology offers, by contrast, is not just philosophical solutions or definitions, but a means to employ these understandings within forms of engagement that yield analytical insight, but which must be realized again and again with respect to each situation, because we live in a changing and varied world of practice.

(Miller, 2005: 3–4)

Despite his skepticism regarding philosophizing about concrete, material things, one of Miller's most profound insights is a deeply philosophical one. Miller promotes a notion of what he calls "the humility of things," or the "somewhat unexpected capacity of objects to fade out of focus and remain peripheral to our vision" (Miller, 2010: 51). Things are important to pay attention to, Miller claims, because all too often they don't call attention to themselves. The world is full of stuff, but most of the stuff in the world doesn't assert itself upon us at every moment. Put another way, we are not conscious of most things in the world unless we actively consider them. Even when in use, most objects bear no significance. Typically I don't think of my shoes when walking around a city street, and I don't think of my pen I use to write in my notebook until their existences—and usually their inadequacies—assert themselves. My shoes aren't something I notice until it starts to snow and I realize I should be wearing boots. My pen is unremarkable until the ink runs out and I can't write any more. It is generally only at the moment when an object proves that it isn't up to its task that we have reason to think of it at all. The idea here is a simple one, but of profound significance when thinking about an object as generally unremarked upon as a baseball glove. A baseball glove seems like any other piece of equipment until it asserts itself as something out of the ordinary, when it fails at its task or when we actively consider the elaborate rituals, practices, and historical debates in which it participates. Concerning this tendency of everyday objects to escape our notice, Miller writes:

> My first theory of things starts with exactly the opposite property of stuff than we would expect. It is not that things are tangible stuff that we can stub our toe against. It is not that they are firm, clear foundations that are opposed to the fluffiness of the images of the mind or abstract ideas. They work by being invisible and unremarked upon, a state they usually achieve by being familiar and taken for granted. Such a perspective seems properly described as material culture since it implies that much of what makes us what we are exists, not through our consciousness or body, but as an exterior environment that habituates and prompts us.

(Miller, 2010: 50–51)

The implication of this "invisibility" of objects is that we generally don't think about the way the material world shapes us. Our typical behaviors—our unconscious ways of being in the world—for the most part depend on objects functioning unnoticed. Paradoxically, however, this insight into materiality also has a decidedly metaphysical dimension. In emphasizing the "humility of things" Miller implicitly evokes the writings of Martin Heidegger, specifically his famous essay "The Thing." Although, according to Heidegger, a thing would seem to demand our attention ("the Old High German word *thing means a gathering, and specifically* a gathering to deliberate on a matter under discussion, a contested matter" (Heidegger, 1975: 175), what actually constitutes "thingness" is that the thing isn't worth discussing. It escapes notice. "In accordance with this," Heidegger argues, "thinging itself is unpretentious, and each present thing, modestly compliant, fits into its own being. Inconspicuously compliant is the thing: the jug and the bench, the footbridge and the plow . . ." (Heidegger, 1975: 180). Most things are simply present in the world. As Heidegger explains in *Being and Time*, a thing reveals itself when its presence is called upon for utility—i.e. when it is necessary to be used as equipment. A hammer is an inert, unremarkable thing until you pick it up to pound a nail and it reveals its being in its use. But it can only be conspicuous—worth thinking about—if it is broken, or missing, or wrong for the purpose, or proves itself to be inadequate. "When something cannot be used—when, for instance, a tool definitely refuses to work—it can be conspicuous only in and for dealings in which something is manipulated" (Heidegger, 1962: 406).

We can see how this particular theory of materiality could be especially pertinent to the baseball glove which is literally—as it were—present at hand. It tends to be inconspicuous and humble in the way Miller describes, even when it is shaping our performance. Nevertheless, it calls to us to engage in certain behaviors, participate in certain routines, and adhere to a certain set of beliefs. When I "put my glove to bed" each winter by oiling it, wrapping it in rubber bands with ball in the pocket, putting it in a pillowcase, and then placing it between my mattress and box spring from November until April, the glove has definitely transformed my habitus. However, though these theories can help us understand the baseball glove, often, even in the work of anthropologists who study baseball, the glove tends to be overlooked as an item of anthropological significance. George Gmelch, the anthropologist and former minor league ballplayer notes that for a game generally obsessed with ritual, superstition, and magical thinking, very little of that obsession concerns fielding and the use of the baseball glove. In his essay "Baseball Magic," Gmelch cites the anthropologist Bronislaw Malinowski and his early twentieth-century work among the Trobriand Islanders in the Western Pacific for the insight that magic, in both industrialized and non-industrialized cultures, tends to coalesce around things over which people have little or no control. "We find magic," Malinowski explains, "wherever the elements of chance and accident, and the emotional play between hope and fear, have a wide and extensive range. We do not find magic wherever the pursuit is certain, reliable, and well under the control of rational methods" (quoted in Gmelch, 1971: 39).

In Malinowski's famous example of the Trobriand Islanders he studied, magical rituals were strategically deployed depending on the danger of the activity and the potential for success:

> Among the Trobrianders, fishing took two forms. In the inner lagoon, fish were plentiful and there was little danger; on the open sea, fishing was dangerous and yields varied widely. Malinowski found that magic was not used in lagoon fishing, where men could rely solely on their knowledge and skill. But when fishing on the open sea, Trobrianders used a great deal of magical ritual to ensure safety and increase their catch.

> (Gmelch, 1978)

Gmelch observes that a similar phenomenon applies in baseball. Pitching and hitting acquire certain rituals and superstitions because the prospect of failure is so much greater. Most successful starting pitchers win only about half of their starts; most batters fail to get a hit 70–75 percent of the time. Fielding, where success is virtually guaranteed, has far fewer rituals and recourse to magical thinking. "The best evidence that players turn to rituals, taboos, and fetishes to control chance and uncertainty," Gmelch observes, "is found in their uneven application."

> They are associated mainly with pitching and hitting—the activities with the highest degree of chance—and not fielding. I met only one player who had any ritual in connection with fielding, and he was an error prone shortstop. Unlike hitting and pitching, a fielder has almost complete control over the outcome of his performance. Once a ball has been hit in his direction, no one can intervene and ruin his chances of catching it for an out (except in the unlikely event of two fielders colliding). Compared with the pitcher or the hitter, the fielder has little to worry about. He knows that, in better than 9.7 times out of 10, he will execute his task flawlessly. With odds like that there is little need for ritual.

(Gmelch, 2001: 142)

Nevertheless, as we shall see, when I turn to some field observations of gloves in use in different communities, they are never completely beneath the notice of those who use them, nor are they completely free of ritual and magic.

Semiotics—A Special Theoretical Case

One of the major fields of anthropological research is linguistic anthropology—the study of how meaning and cultural beliefs are communicated through language. Many linguistic anthropologists study language and language groups from the standpoint of how ideas about identity, gender, race, sexuality, political and group affiliations are expressed through written and oral communication. Where linguistic anthropology overlaps with cultural anthropology, we often talk about it in terms of the loosely defined field of "semiotics." Semiotics (sometimes called semiology) is the study of how intersubjective communication through signs produces meaning.

Semiotics owes its lineage to two key figures, the Swiss linguist Ferdinand de Saussure (1857–1913) and the American philosopher Charles Sanders Peirce (1839–1914). At first blush, the field of semiotics is a complicated one because the early writings are often turgid and dense. Peirce, in particular can be very difficult to read, and often coins confusing and sometimes conflicting neologisms to describe similar ideas. I will attempt to simplify some of the key concepts of semiotics in an effort to suggest how it might help us think through how a baseball glove produces meaning, and in this chapter's "Practicing Anthropology" box, students will have an opportunity to perform their own semiotic analysis to see how it can be useful tool in the anthropologist's tool box.

At its most basic level, semiotics deals with "signs" and how they convey meaning in society (see Breakout Box 3.1). From de Saussure, we get the notion of "structural linguistics" in which the sign is a two-part element consisting of a *signified* (idea, object, or concept) and a *signifier* (a word) to convey that idea. Let's consider the various signifiers for "baseball glove" in the languages currently spoken by Major League Baseball players:

English: Baseball glove
Dutch: Honkbalhandschoen
French: Gant de baseball
German: Baseballhandschuh
Korean: 야구 글러브
Japanese: 野球グラブ
Mandarin: 棒球手套
Portuguese: Luva de baseball
Spanish: Guante de béisbol

What do you notice about this list? Although some of the terms bear a certain resemblance to one another, they are all different. Even in languages with similar origins, there can be derivations. French, German, and Portuguese all borrow the word "baseball" from English, but Spanish and Dutch do not. Hence, one of the first things structural linguistics reminds us is that the signifier for something is *arbitrary*. However, in a language, the signifier and the signified link up, and as long as we participate in a language culture, we can't break that linkage (I can't call the leather thing with finger stalls and webbing "book" or "child" and make any sense to others). The idea of a baseball glove always comes attached to the words "B-A-S-E-B-A-L-L G-L-O-V-E," provided I speak English. If I spoke Dutch, it would come with the word "Honkbalhandschoen," but since I don't speak Dutch, that word conveys little to me. That irrevocable linkage between signifier and signified de Saussure calls the *sign*.

The beauty of language is that, using de Saussure's system, the sign functions in the absence of a referent. I don't need to bring an elephant with me in order to tell you about an elephant—I don't even need to bring a baseball glove. I can communicate a seemingly infinite array of ideas both material and abstract without calling them into existence. However, there are a few deficiencies to de Saussure's structure—some that he himself acknowledges. The first is that this structure of the sign deals only with how meaning is conveyed through language rather than through other means like pictures, sounds, smells, and other forms of signaling. Indeed, de Saussure insisted that his structural definition of the sign was so specific that it really only dealt with speech acts (what he called *parole*) at the expense of considering written language (*langue*). "[Spoken] language," he insisted, "is a system of signs that express ideas, and is therefore comparable to a system of writing, the alphabet of deaf-mutes, symbolic rites, polite formulas, military signals, etc. But it is the most important of all these systems" (de Saussure, 1966: 17). Nevertheless, de Saussure acknowledges that his system of linguistic signs was really only part of a larger, more comprehensive field of signs, the study of which was let to be fully codified:

> A science that studies the life of signs within society is conceivable; it would be a part of social psychology and consequently of general psychology; I shall call it semiology (from Greek semeion 'sign'). Semiology would show what constitutes signs, what laws govern them. Since the science does not yet exist, no one can say what it would be; but it has a right to existence, a place staked out in advance. Linguistics is only a part of the general science of semiology; the laws discovered by semiology will be applicable to linguistics, and the latter will circumscribe a well-defined area within the mass of anthropological facts.
>
>   (de Saussure, 1966: 16)

This quotation from the *Course in General Linguistics* points to a second deficiency of de Saussure's structure of the sign, namely, that it isn't sufficiently anthropological. De Saussure generally doesn't take into account differences in interpretation between different receivers of the communication. For de Saussure, an elephant is an elephant and a baseball glove is a baseball glove, no matter who is hearing about it.

Peirce provides a more flexible and more generous take on the sign by defining it as a three-part structure. As with de Saussure, for Peirce, there is an object or idea I wish to convey and there is a tool I use to convey it, but in Peirce's case, not only are spoken words to be considered appropriate bearers of meaning, but so too are written words, pictures, objects, even colors, sounds, and smells. "A sign is something which stands to somebody for something in some respect or capacity" (Peirce, quoted in Mertz, 2007: 338). What's more, for Peirce, a sign is not complete until its message is received and understood by an "interpretant"— the mental idea created in the mind of an individual. Rachel Mertz, in her analysis of the relationship between semiotics and anthropology writes that "this sign vehicle communicates something by virtue of creating a connection between an object (whatever the sign stands for) and an interpretant (the idea or mental representation now created in our minds" (Mertz, 2007: 338).

Sometimes a sign can represent itself: an elephant is an elephant. Sometimes it represents something else: an elephant on a red, white, and blue background is a sign of the Republican party, while one in green and yellow represents the mascot of the Oakland A's. Context, as well as the other signs available to me and their organization, are key. Peirce gives us a much more generous theory of signs, but he also gives us a far more unstable one, first because signs set off a chain of signification—the Republican elephant doesn't foreclose on me thinking about the Oakland A's one, nor does it stop me from thinking of the chain of Republican presidents from Lincoln to Trump. Signs come weighted with the baggage of society, history, and place. As Keane (2003: 413) writes "Signs give rise to new signs, in an unending process of signification. This is important because, viewed sociologically, it can be taken to entail sociability, struggle, historicity, and contingency."

But this baggage is what makes semiotics invaluable to the cultural anthropologist interested in material objects, for the qualities of an object, its design, its materials, its color, literally everything that makes it *a thing* in the world at a given time and place give it cultural meaning. David Hume believed that human experience was "nothing but a bundle or collection of different perceptions, which succeed each other with an inconceivable rapidity, and are in a perpetual flux and movement" (Hume et al., 1878: 134). What gives us meaning is how those discrete perceptions are joined together under one heading we call "me." The assemblage of qualities I exhibit and experiences I've had: that's my story. Spread over a group of people, that collection of perceptions can rightly be called "culture." Hence, an anthropologically informed semiotics, according to Keane, gives us the language to tell the story of stuff.

> In practice, there is no way entirely to eliminate that factor of co-presence or what we might call "bundling." This points to one of the obvious, but important, effects of materiality: redness cannot be manifest without some embodiment that inescapably binds it to some other qualities as well, which can become contingent but real factors in its social life. Bundling is one of the conditions of possibility for what Kopytoff (1986) and Appadurai (1986) called the "biography" of things, as [qualities] bundled together in any object will shift in their relative value, utility, and relevance across contexts.

(Keane, 2003: 414)

These thumbnail sketches of de Saussure and Peirce radically foreshorten complexity of both men's arguments. Importantly, however, in the latter half of the twentieth century, a group of philosophers and cultural critics inspired by both de Saussure and Peirce try to synthesize their insights and complicate them by introducing the concept of "the social" as a crucial element in the production of meaning. These "post-structuralist" theorists offer, according to Teresa de Lauretis "semiotics concerned to stress the social aspect of signification, its practical, aesthetic, or ideological use in interpersonal communication;

there, meaning is construed as semantic value produced through culturally shared codes" (de Lauretis, 1984: 167).

Arguably one of the most influential of these post-structuralist semioticians was the French theorist Roland Barthes. Although inspired by the sign/signifier dynamic of de Saussure's structural linguistics, Barthes aligned his semiotics with Peirce, who believed both that anything could serve as a sign, and that a sign's meaning was dependent on its interpretant. Hence Barthes expanded his analytical lens to include all manner of objects including advertisements, magazine pages, automobiles, even laundry detergent as signs that told us something vital about the culture that produced them and why they were meaningful to members of a given culture. "We shall therefore take language, discourse, speech, etc., to mean any significant unit or synthesis, whether verbal or visual: a photograph will be a kind of speech for us in the same way as a newspaper article; even objects will become speech, if they mean something" (Barthes, 1984: 111–112). In a series of essays and books, Barthes looked at elements of popular culture through the lens of what he called the two orders of signification. When looking at a text—an image, a movie star's face, or a televised wrestling match— I come to my understanding of the meaning of that thing first by recognizing it for what it is: "At the level of the literal message, the text replies-in a more or less direct, more or less partial manner-to the question: *what is it?*" (Barthes and Heath, 1977: 156). Barthes calls the first order of signification that answers the "what is it" question *denotation*. At the level of denotation, a baseball glove would be a baseball glove. If that's all texts were, however, they would be self-evident, but they would also be terribly boring. Signification is more than simply denotative, which is why we need a further level of signification, where the sign comes to represent meaning—stories, abstract ideas, and cultural concepts. This order of signification Barthes calls *connotation*. Connotative understanding synthesizes all of the available information about a text including any linguistic message it includes and reads it based on a set of "cultural codes," that Barthes claims anyone steeped in a particular society will understand explicitly. But since these cultural codes are so ingrained in our understanding of the text, Barthes claims they need hardly be articulated, "for everyone from a real society always disposes of a knowledge superior to the merely anthropological and perceives more than just the letter" (Barthes and Heath, 1977: 158).

As with Peirce, Barthes believed that the connotations of signs depended on the interpreter in order to decode them properly. The problem with connotations is that since they aren't explicit, they should be inherently unstable. I should be able to read a text, an image, or an object based on my own beliefs and opinions. However, Barthes observed that generally, depending on historical context and sets of cultural assumptions, most texts provoked similar readings and similar responses to most members of a community. "I see very well" what a politically charged photograph in *Paris Match* was meant to signify, Barthes claimed, because he was immersed in a set of cultural assumptions that made those meanings transparent. Barthes called those organizing codes a contemporary society's "myths," and they troubled him, because from another perspective he understood that from a slightly different perspective what we once called myths we would now properly be called "ideology" (Barthes, 1984).

Hence, at the risk of being "merely anthropological," cultural anthropology helps make explicit those cultural beliefs that would otherwise implicitly govern a society's understanding of the world, and semiotics is important to the work anthropology does to help analyze and understand how objects speak to us. Objects take on their meaning depending on how they're actually used and for what purpose. We have already seen how this is embedded in the historical and material specificity of the glove: A zipper-backed 1920s mitt with a Ken-Wel label and a Lou Gehrig signature connotes something anachronistic to a contemporary player, but to a collector, it would connote a lot of money. Likewise, an 11.25-inch glove communicates to a Cuban baseball coach that a middle-aged American plays second base. "Objects become speech," Barthes says, hence we speak the language of second basemen, even across our linguistic differences.

Even at the level of color, the glove is speaking semiotically in a number of registers. The flesh colored-glove Charlie Waite wore in the 1880s was meant to disguise the fact he was wearing it, thereby (purportedly) protecting him from taunts about his manhood. On the other hand (literally), Albert Spalding wore a black glove to advertise that he had a product for sale. Today, a 13-inch pink glove communicates girls' softball even though it would now be legal (and appropriate) for baseball. According to Dave Katz, there is no fundamental difference between a well-made softball glove and a baseball glove other than the aesthetics. But color communicates more than just gender norms. In 1971, MacGregor introduced a line of colored gloves to the game. Although initially, echoing some of the other responses to rules changes regarding the glove, a few managers objected, notably the Mets' Gil Hodges. But in the years following the colored gloves' introductions, the use of a colored glove—especially a multi-colored one—became a shorthand for Major League players of color. As Noah Liberman explains:

> When Manny Trillo had the back of his tan glove dyed black in the late seventies, he set off a fashion trend that evolves to this day. First Latino infielders followed his lead . . . [N]ow you can find factory-made multicolored gloves at every position, although glove makers suggest that Latino and black players still lead the league in fashion.

(Liberman, 2003: 93)

Breakout Box 3.1: Practicing Anthropology:
Semiotic Analysis

In Roland Barthes' essay "Myth Today," he claims that many signs, particularly those we see in popular culture, are at their heart ideological, i.e. promoting some agenda. He argues that the task of the "semiologist," the reader of signs, is to go beyond the denotative and connotative meanings of signs—which he claims present themselves "naturally" or automatically to most readers, to a third level of meaning, where we see how—and more importantly why—the "myths" evoked by the sign have become naturalized by social and historical processes. "If one wishes to connect a mythical schema to a general history," he insists, "to explain how it corresponds to the interests of a definite society, in short, to pass from semiology to ideology, it is obviously at the level of the third type of focusing that one must place oneself: it is the reader of myths himself who must reveal their essential function" (Barthes, 1984: 127).

Take a look at the cover from the April 21, 1945 edition of the *Saturday Evening Post* by Stevan Dohanos called "Island Game" (Figure 3.3).

It is a provocative image, with many features to unpack, interrogate, and analyze (which are all ways academics say "interpret"). Its context is the US occupation of a number of islands in the Pacific theater in the years during and after World War II and the type of "baseball diplomacy" (National Security Archive, n.d.) that has characterized a number of US encounters with other nations dating from Spalding's 1888 baseball "World Tour" designed to make the rest of the globe baseball players and customers (Lamster, 2006), to the decades-old struggle over the national character of baseball waged between the US and Cuba, culminating with the exhibition game President Obama attended between the Tampa Bay Rays and the Cuban national team at the Latinoamericano stadium in Havana (Eastman, NSA). The influential anthropologist, George Peter Murdock, who studied the Micronesian Chuuk (formerly Truk) state in the 1940s, wrote about this period and episodes like the one displayed on the Post cover in an essay called "Waging Baseball in Truk." In 1990 Bill Brown revisited this period and Murdock's work in an essay called, "Waging Baseball, Playing War: Games of American Imperialism," which appeared in the journal *Cultural Critique*. Whereas Murdock generally celebrates the inter-cultural baseball games as a positive example of cross-cultural exchange, going so far as to note how the Chuukese adapt the game to their own ritual practices ("The Trukese know all the rules, even those about balks and infield flies . . . The players practice almost daily and observe all the sexual and other taboos which they used to precede war" [Murdock, 1965: 292]) Brown

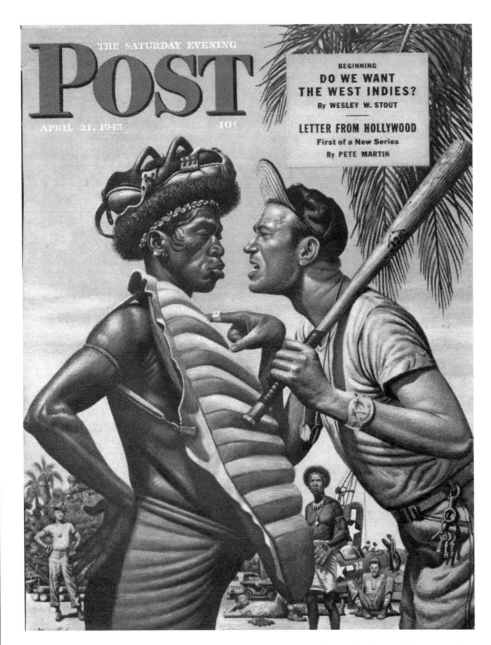

Figure 3.3 Saturday Evening Post, **April 21, 1945.** (*Source*: Cover by Stevan Dohanos.)

has decidedly more pessimistic take on these episodes: "Baseball textually suppresses the violence of imperialist aggression," he claims:

No mention is made of the fact that Japan, in 1914, seized and annexed the islands, which served as a naval base in World War II until the allied invasion; we're told that an all-Truk team defeated a team from the American Navy in 1947, but not that the navy is there as part of the American occupation.

(Brown, 1990–91: 53)

Clearly there is much to debate about the episode in baseball diplomacy depicted in this image, but is also an image ripe for semiotic analysis.

As an assignment, have the students read either "The Rhetoric of the Image" or "Myth Today" by Roland Barthes and ask them to do a semiotic analysis of Dohanos' illustration. What are the denotative features of the image? Can they catalog them? How are they organized? What parts are emphasized? What connotations are conveyed? What historical context is needed to "read" the image? How do we interpret the image from a contemporary standpoint? Following Barthes, what "myths" or ideologies does this image evoke? Finally—since after all you are reading a book about baseball gloves—how might the baseball gloves depicted in the illustration change the interpretation?

Suggested Reading

Brown, Bill. "Waging Baseball, Playing War: Games of American Imperialism," *Cultural Critique* 17, (1990–91): 51–78.

Elias, Robert. *The Empire Strikes Out: How Baseball Sold U.S. Foreign Policy and Promoted the American Way Abroad.* New York: The New Press, 2010.

Murdock, George Peter. "Waging Baseball on Truk," In *Culture and Society: Twenty-Four Essays*, 290–293. Pittsburgh: University of Pittsburgh Press, 1965.

Liberman provides ample anecdotal evidence of this connection between color and race, and while the link between the race and ethnicity and the color of a player's glove is not a hard and fast rule. We can see plenty of similar examples today. Watch a Red Sox game for the distinctive dance done by its outfield trio of Mookie Betts, Jackie Bradley, Jr., and Andrew Benitendi. Look past their signature moves at their gloves. Betts and Bradley Jr. (both African American players) have distinctive multi-color gloves while Benitendi (who is white) wears basic brown. Likewise, in a YouTube video, a young white player demonstrates how to "pimp" a glove with long red laces, but he claims that the "dreadlocks" he creates are too "ostentatious" for him. While none of these signs are individually racially coded, bundled together, "dreadlocks," "ostentatious," and "pimping" portray a stereotyped image of black culture coalescing around the material rhetoric of the long, bright red laces of the glove.

Figure 3.4 **Steve McQueen in** *The Great Escape.* (*Source*: Getty Images.)

Popular Culture

As a semiotic analysis can help us see, one of the ways gloves take on meaning is through their appearance in popular culture. throughout much of the last century when baseball gloves appear in the mass media they do so as short-hand for sets of ideas and beliefs about "The American Character" (Elias, 2010). Of course, in a nation as heterogeneous and diverse as the United States, the notion that there could be something definable as the American character is inherently problematic. Nevertheless, authors from Alexis de Tocqueville to Frederick Jackson Turner and beyond have endeavored to define it, and of course every politician and US president has articulated a vision of what these characteristics mean. Baseball has always been a convenient way of providing a lens on what it means to be American. In the film *Field of Dreams*, the radical author Terrence Mann, played by James Earl Jones makes this link explicit. Baseball is not only quintessentially American, it is the ideal of America's best self:

> The one constant through all the years, Ray, has been baseball. America has rolled by like an army of steamrollers. It's been erased like a blackboard, rebuilt, and erased again. But baseball has marked the time. This field, this game: it's a part of our past . . . It reminds of us of all that once was good and that could be again.

(Robinson, 1989, Field of Dreams)

Field of Dreams articulates a teleologically oriented vision of an America constantly evolving toward the "more perfect union" enshrined in the Constitution. Through teamwork, ingenuity, hard work, and fair play (albeit with some bending of the rules), Americans and American democracy will triumph.

When the glove appears in popular culture it is often a metonymy of these ideas. In a number of scenes in *The Great Escape* Steve McQueen's character Virgil Hilts uses his baseball glove as part of his process of solving the problem of getting out of the film's German prison camp (see Figure 3.4). At first he pretends to play with his glove and ball to test the attentiveness of the prison camp guards and then, most iconically, he takes his glove into "the cooler" with him where he uses the repetitive gesture of throwing a baseball against the prison wall and catching it on the rebound as the spur to his thought process as he plots his escape under the wire. Indeed, despite the fact that he is recaptured at the end of the movie, in the film's final sequence fellow prisoners toss Hilts his glove as he is led once more into the cooler and *The Great Escape* closes with him popping a ball into his glove to illustrate the indomitability of the American spirit and the continuing commitment to ingenuity and inventiveness. It is as though the film is saying that an American could resist the German army solely with a baseball glove and a ball. This image is so iconic that it is evoked in various pop culture mash ups as Maggie Simpson's escape from a day care facility in *The Simpsons* episode "A Streetcar Named Marge" and the super-spy Sterling Archer's escape from captivity in a space station in the *Archer* episode "Space Race." In each of these references, the baseball glove is used as a means of conveniently identifying and commenting on a certain brand of distinctly American problem-solving in the face of adversity and commenting on that legacy.

Part of that discourse on American ingenuity points to another connotation embodied in the baseball glove, one which we saw in the marketing materials cited at the beginning of this chapter: the notion of America's commitment to craftsmanship and the intimate relationship between problem-solving and problem-finding, technique and expression, play and work. From the original

Figure 3.5 **Fidel Castro with Baseball Glove (1959).** (*Source*: STR/Stringer/Getty Images.)

hacking of the glove to Bill Doak's innovation of webbing to the Latina family's work with Rawlings and the Storey family's multi-generation stewardship of the Nokona company, the mythos of the glove has included a notion of American craftsmanship passed down from generation to generation. Rawlings has its "100 years of Rawlings' glove-making craftsmanship," Wilson touts "Master Craftsman" Shigeaki Aso, the Japanese Glove Guru brought from Japan to the United States to design and break-in gloves.

Richard Sennett, in his book on craftsmanship sees this idea as something inextricably tied to the notion of the American character "Thomas Jefferson's democratic celebration of the American farmer-yeoman or skilled artisan stands on the same ground, the practical man being able to judge how well government is built because he understands building" (Sennett, 2008: 269). This idea of craftsmanship extends from the material production of the glove to the use of the glove in the field. Whereas in batting where success and failure are so dependent on chance and hence superstition and magic ritual predominate in player's practice (Gmelch, 1971). The glove tends to be rhetorically linked to the realm of hard work. "Glove work" and "plying the leather" are two common terms for competent fielding, while the phrase "the tools of ignorance" are ironically applied to the catcher's gear in reference to the putatively low intelligence of players who would choose such a hazardous and potentially injurious position.

The rhetoric of craftsmanship is also a rhetoric about baseball's claim on American consciousness. Whereas other sports equipment often gestures to technological innovation and futurism, the baseball glove's rhetoric of craftsmanship points to myths about the labor of working class artisans, particularly those who emigrate to the United States and embrace "the American dream."

Of course the glove can also represent an interruption in those characteristics of what it means to be American. Perhaps the most famous baseball glove in US literature is the one Holden Caufield owns in J.D. Salinger's *Catcher in The Rye*, the glove once owned by Holden's brother Allie. "My brother Allie had this left-handed fielder's mitt," Holden explains:

> He was left-handed. The thing that was descriptive about it, though, was that he had poems written all over the fingers and the pocket and everywhere. In green ink. He wrote them on it so that he'd have something to read when he was in the field and nobody was up at bat.

> (Salinger, 2001: 49)

The left-handedness, the poems on the glove, the notion that a boy would be in the ballfield reading during the lulls in the game—all of these add up to Allie's radical outsiderness and the disruption his death causes in Holden's existence. The glove becomes a symbol of everything keeping Holden from the "phoniness" of the American dream.

> The passage in *The Catcher In The Rye* in which Holden is writing a paper describing his brother's baseball glove has always stuck in my memory. I myself wrote a paper in high school describing the process of waking up a glove in the springtime after it had been dormant for the winter.

> (VTMSBL player)

Finally, the glove can function as a point of resistance to American hegemony. As the anthropologist Ben Eastman (2013) writes, in Cuba, there is a complicated relationship with the game of baseball, where the adoption of America's national pastime serves as an implicit cooptation and point of resistance against the ongoing embargo. Success in baseball, on an international stage, is effectively an announcement of resistance against the embargo and the United States. When I traveled in Cuba with a team of young baseball players, two weeks after President Obama had attended a game at the Estadio Latinoamericano in Havana on March 21, 2016, that pride in baseball was everywhere in evidence, both on the youth ballfields and in the proliferation of images of Fidel Castro playing baseball either in his traditional fatigues or in a baseball uniform (see Figure 3.5). Indeed, when we were invited to tour the Estadio Latinoamericano, the baseball exhibit in the entryway is dominated by a striking and immense drawing of a smiling Fidel with a baseball glove on his hand. As I stood in front of the drawing, it occurred to me that the 2016 date in the corner suggested that it was completed specifically for the US President who had passed by this spot mere days before. The message the glove was sending was clear: This is Cuba's game, as much as it is yours.

Meaning in the Field

Cultural anthropologists are interested in theoretical questions, how meaning is produced in abstract terms and through the texts of popular culture, but they are also curious about less deterministic meanings—i.e. how users actually interact with an object in the real word. For individuals who regularly interact with the baseball glove as a material object and for whom the glove has a special significance, we can sort them into a number of loosely defined subgroups including practitioners (players), enthusiasts (collectors), and makers and shapers (glove manufacturers and "glove doctors"). These groups are likely to overlap one another. Players and former players may also be collectors. Glove manufacturers may also have been players, etc. We have had an opportunity to consider each of these groups throughout the book, but it is clear that, of the three groups, players are the most likely to have developed the most intricate set of practices and beliefs regarding gloves since, as a group, they are the ones who interact most directly and most often with them as a piece of equipment. The rituals of break-in, the "feel" in the hand, and the effectiveness of their play are likely the driving concerns for this group. Despite Gmelch's insistence that fielding typically escapes the type of magical thinking we associate with some cultural practices, including practices specific to baseball, it is clear both from my fieldwork with players and from interviews with Major Leaguers, superstitions abound. "I'm super superstitious," Dansby Swanson says in a video on Wilson's website "I usually name my gloves . . . The one from the [College] world series was named Charlotte" (Wilson Sporting Goods, n.d.). Hall of Fame shortstop Ozzie Smith, would, under certain circumstances, let players touch his glove, but only within certain limits: "I would allow people to pick it up unless a guy was in an awful slump. 'Get your hand off that. Don't bring me that problem!'" (quoted in Liberman, 2003: 115–116). ESPN baseball analyst Tim Kurkjian reports that Hall of Famer Roberto Alomar once went to his locker to discover someone had touched his glove:

> "Someone's hand has been inside my glove," he said. He looked around the clubhouse and asked, "Who put my glove on?" He was not happy. "You can't put someone else's glove on, you mess up the pocket, the feel, everything," he said. "If anyone puts my glove on, I can tell right away. It has a different feel."

> (Kurkjian, 2002)

These superstitions and rituals tend to hold true at the amateur levels of baseball as well. Beyond the usual routines of players who diligently put a ball in the pocket between defensive innings to maintain the glove's shape and those who always put their gloves in the same place in the dugout, there are players who put their gloves in a special bag during and after the game, those who put their glove in their cap (or vice versa), and of course those who would never let another player use their glove for the way it changes the fit, or feel, or even the temperature and moisture content inside.

Players are also most likely to talk about the meaning of the glove in terms of intergenerational and peer to peer exchange. These types of exchanges in which ritual practices are taught to other members of the community are of special interest to cultural anthropologists, both for what they tell us about a given society's history and what they can tell us about the present day.

> Although rituals are often perceived as being 'traditional,' passed on in the same form from generation to generation, the fact is that rituals are an ongoing human activity and must be re-created every time they are performed. Hence rituals are subject to both intentional and unintentional change.

> (Dubisch, 2012: 279)

Meaning is both preserved and transformed by the passage of an object or a practice from one generation to another, and the glove is a particularly meaningful object in this regard.

A player in the Vermont Men's Senior Baseball League summarized that significance in this way:

My favorite baseball glove of all time was my dad's Wilson Wilbur Wood model ... in fact, it's amazing the memories an old baseball glove can bring. I always wanted to use that glove, but it was too big. I totally looked up to my dad, loved playing catch with him and loved to watch him play softball. As I grew up and into it, I always felt such a connection and sense of pride in using that glove. We all go through different phases in life, but years later as I picked up baseball again, it may be no coincidence that a Wilson is the only glove I've had as an adult. A few years back, I bought an old Wilbur Wood model on eBay and had Mr. Wood sign it for my father. It hangs in a case in my parent's house as a reminder of the connection a simple piece of leather can create.

At the same time, the baseball glove can represent the disruption of generational exchange. In *Field of Dreams*, the protagonist, Ray Kinsella, pegs the break with his father to the moment when he stopped playing baseball with him. "Can you believe that? An American boy refusing to play catch with his father." And in a sense, the entire resolution of the film and its intergenerational conflict between the Vietnam era counterculture embodied by Ray and the previous, conservative generation of his father is predicated on Ray encountering the ghost of his father, donning a baseball glove, and asking, "Hey, Dad. Do you want to have a catch?" (Robinson, 1989, *Field of Dreams*).

In part because of the role generational exchange plays in players' feelings about a glove's meaning, and because many players were given their glove at a young age, the glove conjures for them a sense of place, the significance of origin, home, and belonging. In many of the interviews I conducted with players, it was noteworthy that the story of the glove was often explicitly connected with a home town. "It brings me back," these middle-aged men will say, as though the glove were a time machine capable of transporting them, bodily, to another time and place.

Another subset of people for whom the glove takes on special meaning are collectors. As my friend Luis Vivanco and his colleagues write in their cultural anthropology textbook, "The most powerful examples of objects that change meaning when they pass into different hands come from the situation where an anthropologist or collector buys objects" (Welsch and Vivanco, 2016: 402). For collectors, a glove's meaning comes down to its connection to history and its monetary value rather than its use on the field or personal memoir. There are a wide variety of resources on the internet for glove collectors and a number of thriving communities who exchange stories, photos and sales reports.

For the collectors, the material features of the glove, the historical significance, and the evolution of design dominate the conversation. These communities, including baseballglovecollector.com and vintagebaseballgloveforum.com, are extremely knowledgeable and are an invaluable resource for researchers interested in the material history and evolution of the glove. These collectors not only know what glove Steve McQueen was likely wearing in *The Great Escape* (a Rawlings RR or KK model with a doctored webbing); they can also explain why the glove in *The Shawshank Redemption* is likely inappropriate for the setting of the film. But the meaning of the glove to them is different than it is to a player. The French philosopher, Jean Baudrillard, in an essay on antiques, claims that the significance of objects deemed collectibles is that their meaning no longer derives from their use value, but rather from their ability to point to a historical moment or a specific player.

> There is a whole range of objects—including unique, baroque, folkloric, exotic and antique objects—that seem to fall outside the system we have been examining. They appear to run counter to the requirements of func- tional calculation, and answer to other kinds of demands such as witness, memory, nostalgia or escapism. It is tempting to treat them as survivals from the traditional, symbolic order. Yet for all their distinctiveness, these objects do play a part in modernity, and that is what gives them a double meaning. The antique object no longer has any practical application, its role being merely to signify.
>
> (Baudrillard, 1996: 77–78)

A glove that has passed onto the status of a collectible is no longer used to play the game—and hence pragmatic concerns about its use disappear, a distinction Rob Storey was quick to point out when I showed him a 1940s model Nokona with a small hole in the back. If I wanted to play with it, they'd likely stitch it up, but if I wanted to display the glove, they would advise against doing anything otherwise it would appear "cobbled on" and lose its value as a collectible (inter- view with Rob Storey, 2016). Despite this sense that a glove might lose value if were to be repaired with contemporary materials, for many collectors, financial reward is an important concern but not the predominant one. Instead, many of the discussions on the collecting sites focus on historical significance and how generally non-lucrative the hobby is.

Yet another group we have already examined are the makers and shapers, the manufacturers, "Glove Doctors," "Glove Gurus" and the like. This is generally the smallest of the subgroups for whom the baseball glove has special significance, but the one that has the largest financial stake in the sale and modification of sporting goods. Curiously, they are also the group who is most likely to disagree with one another and find fault in the work of their fellows. For manufacturers, fellow makers are also competitors; for the glove doctors and people who break-in gloves professionally, different glove designs represent challenges and impediments to their work. Noah Liberman profiles Fran Fleet, the "Sandalady," who has plenty of criticism for the glovemakers whose products she works with:

> Nokona's leathers are too soft, she says. Wilson's earlier A2000s had thumb loops that didn't tighten far enough . . . "The guy who invented the Basket Web for Rawlings"—renowned designer Rollie Latina, actually, with nearly thirty patents to his name—"didn't know what he was doing. Every time you catch with it it stretches, and there's no way to tighten it."
>
> (Liberman, 2003: 87)

And whereas players and collectors tend to be generous with their knowledge, even if that knowledge is contradictory, the glove doctors often jealously guard their secrets. Fleet "gets testy when a reporter gets technical with his questions" about her glove potion. When I interviewed Dave Katz, he studiously refused to tell me anything about the details of his break-in process, including whether it had required him to design any of his own equipment for his business. "You can imagine whatever you want," he told me when I pushed him on his process.

Finally, there is the group that perhaps encapsulates all of these other subgroups: fans. There is an extensive body of literature on sports fandom from an anthropological perspective (Bourdieu, 1999; Shore, 1994), and while fans have a number of ritualized and ethnographic practices and behaviors that have been well studied in a variety of sports from football (American) (Miller, 1997) to football (English) (Armstrong, 1998), baseball fans exhibit a curious behavior with regard to the glove: they bring them to the game in anticipation of making a catch. That is to say, the glove allows the spectator to be part of the game:

> The wearing of baseball uniforms extends into the spectator stands as well, where fans often show up with baseball caps, gloves and even the uniform shirts of their teams. A highlight of any game, followed closely by television cameras, is what is called "grandstand fielding." Spectators compete with one another to catch fly balls hit into the stands. Such catches are greeted with great cheers from the stands.
>
> (Shore, 1994: 357)

I caught a foul pop with my first glove, my Manny Trillo model, at Fenway Park when I was in 4th grade: Tuesday, September 25th, 1984 (Baseball Reference is a great thing). It was the 7th inning of a 14-6 win by the Sox over the Blue Jays and I spied an empty seat about 4 rows off the field down the third base line, so I left my family and snuck down to sit by myself in the empty red box seat. I happened to be decked out in full Red Sox uniform with one of those cheap plastic souvenir helmets on my head. A few pitches later a high popup looked like it was heading in my direction, so to negate the height advantage of the adults around me I stood on my seat and reached for the sky. As I could see the pearl descend through the outstretched hands around me I believed I had a chance. Thwapp! I felt the impact, opened my Manny Trillo model and there was the beautiful pearl – the ball seemed to glow against the dark brown leather like only a major league ball could. All the grownups around me slapped me on the back in congratulations. I turned around and my mother was laughing hysterically in amazement. The next pitch to the Blue Jays third baseman (who was pinch-hitting), Kelly Gruber, was hit out over the Monster for a HR and the Gruber's first major league hit. A few outs later an older gentleman tapped me on the shoulder and asked me to sign the front of his program—Kelly Gruber's dad.

(VTMSBL player)

Value

For each of these subcultures, the baseball glove has a value. "Value" is a special category of meaning with its own theories, ideologies, and debates, and the critique of value has a rich and complicated history touching not only on economics and the theories of wages, rents, and commodity exchange that develop in the eighteenth and nineteenth centuries, but also on the fields of philosophy and moral judgment. When we say an object is valuable, we may be saying that we have put a price on it, but we could also be saying that we feel strong sentiment for or attachment to it. Sometimes those two ideas coincide, sometimes they diverge. In 2002, the journal *Cultural Anthropology* dedicated a special issue to "Value in Circulation" to explore the "value of value as a theoretical concept and mode of analysis" offering students of culture "a multidimensional rubric for critical transdisciplinary inquiry" (Eiss and Pedersen, 2002: 283). Put another way, from the standpoint of cultural anthropology, value is an important window onto how people understand material objects, the feelings they have about them and the social relationships that are mediated through them. Recognizing how deeply intertwined the notion of value is with the work of cultural anthropology, the editors of "Value in Circulation" address the multiple ways the term has been employed over the last 300 years:

To embark upon the study of value is to enter a field well-trodden by others. From Smith and Ricardo to Marx and Mauss, and by way of Simmel and Saussure, the category has been used in varied ways to illuminate ethical, economic, aesthetic, logical, linguistic, and political dimensions of human life. Over the course of the twentieth century, divergent understandings of value have often been expressed in terms of dyadic distinctions: Value is about measure or meaning; it is material or symbolic, secular or sacred, abstract or concrete, individual or collective, qualitative or quantitative, global or local. Its origins and content can be found in either production or in exchange, in structure or in process. To inquire into value often has meant to choose between focusing on social relations or objects, the makeup of persons or of polities, systems of meaning or patterns of action.

(Eiss and Pedersen, 2002: 283)

As Eiss and Pedersen reveal, value is a complicated set of social relations centering on how objects take on meaning in the world. For our purposes, the most important of the economic and social theorists they cite to help us understand how a baseball glove assumes value as one of its many meanings is Karl Marx. In a famous passage from the first volume of *Capital*, Marx identifies what he calls the "mystical character" of commodities "abounding in metaphysical subtleties and theological niceties." Namely, an object has a pragmatic use value—a baseball glove is good for catching a baseball. But it also has an exchange value, what it is sold for on the marketplace. The problem, as Marx saw it, is that while the use value of an object was more or less rational and self-evident and more or less stable—any glove made in the last 60 years will do roughly the same job of catching a baseball—its exchange value as a commodity was irrational and wildly fluctuating, deriving as it did from sets of social relationships far removed from the pragmatic use value of an object.

Marx sees this divergence—and the fact that people accept it—as tantamount to the belief in gods and spirits:

There, the existence of the things *quâ* commodities, and the value relation between the products of labour which stamps them as commodities, have absolutely no connection with their physical properties and with the material relations arising therefrom. There it is a definite social relation between men, that assumes, in their eyes, the fantastic form of a relation between things.

(Marx and Engels, 1915: 83)

"Commodity fetishism," as Marx saw it, was what convinced people that value was inherent in an object apart from the labor and raw materials invested in its manufacture.

What, then, is the value of a baseball glove? For the most part, a baseball glove can be bought new for anywhere between $20 and $600. That is an extraordinary range for an object that, at the low and high ends of the cost scale, is not fundamentally different in terms of design and function. While there are certainly differences in the type and quality of the material used in the production of the glove, those differences hardly account for the discrepancy. Consider the Rawlings Heart of the Hide model—long the standard for the industry and the glove many professionals use. Without too much shopping around, one can find a Heart of the Hide Glove for $175–$200: expensive for a piece of sporting equipment, but compared to Rawlings' top of the line Gold Glove model at $500, a moderately priced glove. But if we are to take Glove Doctor Dave Katz at his word in his assessment of the difference in quality between these two gloves "anything over a Heart of the Hide is 100% marketing" (interview with the author).

For Marx, the only way to make sense of discrepancies in value was through appealing to people's belief in the relative costs of commodities as real, hence his insistence on the term "fetishism." Just as in religious practices in which adherents accord powers and values to everyday objects on the basis of deeply held beliefs, in the marketplace, consumers fervently believe that one model of glove is worth substantially more than another. It may not be "100% marketing," as Katz claims, but marketing is part of the social relationship that informs our understanding of value in the world. When the French designer Hermès marketed a $14,000 hand-sewn calf-skin glove (Chin, 2014), it is almost certain that no one buying it would do so believing that it would make them 100 times more effective as a shortstop than buying a perfectly serviceable glove for $140. Indeed, it is hard to imagine someone even using a Hermès glove, given how much it costs. Instead, a customer buys a $14,000 glove as a result of a whole range of cultural discourses around luxury, wealth, and status far removed from the use value of a glove.

But an idea of value can have significant impacts on the cultural reality of the game. In America, baseball has always had an identity crisis with regards to issues of race and class. On the one hand, it was an egalitarian game that anyone could play, as long as one had a stick and ball. On the other hand, it was a "gentleman's game," in which the codes of white, male masculinity were upheld and normalized. And although there were black professional baseball players in the nineteenth century, from that point until 1947, when Jackie Robinson joined the Brooklyn Dodgers, Major League Baseball was rigidly segregated. Today, the cost of baseball equipment is a proxy for much of the complicated racial history of the game. Simply put, the cost of a baseball glove precludes many economically under-privileged players and people of color from taking up the game. There has been a sizeable body of research on the dwindling participation of African Americans in baseball (Brown and Bennett, 2015; Cooper et al., 2012; Ogden, 2004; Nightengale, 2012), and throughout these analyses, there is a consistent thread: US players of color are precluded from playing because of the costs involved including equipment. In their essay "Baseball is Whack," Bandon Brown and Gregg Bennett interview a number of African American players, and the consensus among them is that equipment, among other costs, is an impediment to participation:

> Many of the participants noted that baseball was either too expensive to play, or that the style of the game was inconvenient for play (i.e., requiring nine players on each team, or requiring a baseball bat and glove, instead of requiring a single ball and hoop) . . . for African Americans to excel at baseball, a financial commitment is needed. Several participants noted that this financial inconvenience served as a reason for baseball's (un) popularity. That is, because baseball is not convenient to access, its popularity has dwindled.

> (Brown and Bennett, 2015: 12)

As many of these studies argue, the barrier to entry set up by the cost of equipment starts a vicious circle: Since the cost of equipment is an impediment to participation, fewer African American players participate at an entry level in youth baseball. Since fewer African Americans participate in youth baseball, fewer African Americans participate in the pros. Since fewer African Americans participate in the pros, fewer African American players see themselves represented in the game, setting up yet another disincentive to participation. Hence, the cost of a baseball glove is integrally intertwined with the diversity of the game.

Value therefore is anthropologically significant as a bearer of meaning because it tells us at a given historical moment what we believe about an object and its relative importance in our cultural practices. As Igor Kopytoff reminds us, the value of a commodity like a baseball glove is of fundamental importance to understanding its "biography."

> A commodity is a thing that has use value and that can be exchanged in a discrete transaction for a counterpart, the very fact of exchange indicating that the counterpart has, in the immediate context, an equivalent value. The counterpart is by the same token also a commodity at the time of exchange. The exchange can be direct or it can be achieved indirectly by way of money, one of whose functions is as a means of exchange. Hence, anything that can be bought for money is at that point a commodity, whatever the fate that is reserved for it after the transaction has been made.

> (Kopytoff, 1986: 68–69)

One of the idiosyncracies of commodity exchange is that while most objects follow regular patterns of valuation within the logic of the personal experience of value in the marketplace—even a $14,000 Hermès glove makes sense within the context of the French fashion world—at times certain objects take on out-sized value on the basis of a set of historical contingencies. As we have seen, a glove can become valuable because its design or its model number are histori-cally significant or because of the endorsement it bears as was the case of the Babe Ruth and Lou Gehrig models cited in Chapter 2, but a glove can also take on value by virtue of who wore or was purported to wear it—and when. The stakes of this sort of value can be extraordinarily high. In 1999, at a sports mem-orabilia auction, Sotheby's offered "a game-used Mickey Mantle glove, adver-tised as 'circa 1960,'" meaning that it had been worn during the Yankees legend's prime. "After some furious bidding, the glove went to '61*' director Billy Crystal for a whopping $239,000" (O'Keefe, 2003). The problem was that the glove Crystal bought was ultimately discovered to have been produced much later than 1960—the model in question wasn't in production until 1964—and thus came from late in Mantle's career when he was on the decline. In a *Forbes* essay about the auction and subsequent discovery of the glove's prove-nance, some collectors felt that Crystal had paid too much, by at least $100,000, but baseball glove expert Dennis Esken instead gets at the heart of the "mysti-cal" nature of value and the power of belief: "This isn't like real estate—you can't compare the price of a glove to a similar glove. Every auction is different. This glove is worth whatever Billy Crystal thinks it is worth" (O'Keefe, 2003).

At least Crystal bought a glove that actually belonged to the player purported to have worn it. In 2012, Irving Scheib tried to pass off a nineteenth-century workman's-style glove as the childhood glove of Babe Ruth and sell it for $200,000. In a widely reported story, Scheib bought a nineteenth-century glove for $750 on eBay and then invented an elaborate story that the glove had been Ruth's as a child and that Ruth himself had given the glove to the actor Robert Young with a handwritten note that Scheib had forged. "I sold a baseball glove falsely claiming it was a Babe Ruth glove, and it was not, your honor," Mr. Scheib told Judge Robert P. Patterson Jr. "I feel horrible about it, but those are the facts" (Weiser, 2012). Scheib could have faced 20 years in prison for wire fraud, but instead was sentenced to "two years' probation and a $25,000 fine, and was barred from peddling sports memorabilia until his sentence is completed" (Gearty and McShane, 2012).

What the stories of Mantle's and Ruth's gloves reveal is a curious aspect of how value is assessed through the fetishization of objects. As Peter Stallybrass and Rosalind Jones write in an essay about the fetishized power of the glove in Renaissance Europe, Western cultures tend to put themselves above the idea of the magical power of the fetish. "The fetish," they write, "came into being above all as a term of religious abuse, by which Europeans rejected objects that were attributed with animating powers" (Stallybrass and Jones, 2001: 114). Nevertheless, gloves took on special status as an object taken directly from the hand of the wearer, in much the same way that a letter or signature is written in the hand of the person who writes it. As such, they argue, gloves became a part of those who wore them. "Gloves materialized the power of people to be condensed and absorbed into things and of things to become persons" (Stallybrass and Jones, 2001: 116).

At the same time that a commodity like a baseball glove participates in a set of economic discourses, a crucial element of its biography is that it is a deeply personal item of individual use. What would I pay today for a Ted Williams model fielder's glove like the one I remember from my youth, assuming I could find the exact same model? Could I honestly say I would even buy one, given the glove I use today and how its size is fitted to my current position? It's doubtful that I would pay anything for such a glove. At the same time, I can't imagine any amount of money would make me part with my childhood glove. For Kopytoff, this is the curious paradox of an object's biography. There is a divergence between monetary value and personal value, and

> in any society, the individual is often caught between the cultural structure of commoditization and his own personal attempts to bring a value order to the universe of things. Some of this clash between culture and individual is inevitable, at least at the cognitive level.

> (Kopytoff, 1986: 76)

Ultimately, in interviewing players about their gloves, what emerges is how personal they are to the user—arguably more so than any other piece of sporting equipment, and how much that personal value trumps all other values for the user. That value derives from a combination of factors, both sentiment and playability:

> I have only had my current glove for a year and it is not my glove by choice. My glove I had all through middle and high school disappeared a few years back. I am not a conspiracy theorist, but I really think someone walked off with it. I know where I had last placed it and when I returned a few hours later, it was gone. Though it's been about 6 years since it disappeared, I still am continually keeping an eye out in the park for someone walking around with it. Each spring and fall I check the supply shed at the park to see if it has been turned it. I will never give up hope that it will return.

> (VTMSBL player)

Conclusion: Nostalgia and My Daughter's Gloves

It's a secular country, so we forget: baseball contains primeval images, and
we return to the game because of them, not because we are athletes. We go
back to the memory of ourselves . . . The smell from within the pocket of
an oiled glove is as dizzying as tomato leaves or lemon flowers.

(Richard Grossinger, "The Baseball Junkies,"
quoted in Light, 2005: 378)

Of course the one area of meaning that until now has been implicit in our
approach to the baseball glove has been "nostalgia," a longing for the past.
Nostalgia is, of course where many of the memoirs about baseball go, and where
many of the interviews I did with players, glovemakers, parents, and children
ended up. The glove reminds people of something they have lost: youth, prom-
ise, vitality, simplicity, innocence, and—ultimately—home. Much has been made
of baseball's evocation of home, from George Carlin's classic "Baseball vs. Football" comedy routine ("In baseball the object is to go home! And to be safe!—
I hope I'll be safe at home!"), to the various evocations of "Home" in Ken Burns'
documentary *Baseball*. The game makes all sorts of rhetorical evocations of
home, national origins, and sense of place, and the glove often stands as a metaphor for the home that people long to return to. "Scratch the surface of nine
out of ten men of my generation," Christopher Buckley writes in an essay appro-
priately called "Nostalgia: The 1950s and My Mitts," "and they can tell you about
their favorite baseball mitt or mitts from their youth" (Buckley, 2008: 94).

Nostalgia can be a dangerous thing. Often times what we remember about
the "home" of the past—the shining city on the hill, or the America we want to
make great again is a distorted image of what home once was, seen through
rose-colored glasses—or a fun house-mirror, pick your cliché. The reality is that
the times and places we associate with home was just as fractious, complex and
contentious as our own moment right now, and the sites of nostalgic longings
were often not particularly felicitous places for people suffering under oppression
or living as second-class citizens. Hence, as a number of theorists (Hutcheon,
1998; Jameson, 1991; Stewart, 1988) have argued, nostalgia tends to have an
ideological element. What we reach for in nostalgia is a packaged sense of
belonging to a certain era or locale that perhaps was never ours to begin with.
In nostalgia, we construct an imagined ideal that informs our real engagement
with the world.

Nostalgia, therefore, helps construct value—the value of belonging to an "imagined community" to borrow Benedict Anderson's famous term for the compelling
fiction that is national identity (Anderson, 1991), or what Andreas Huyssen

(2003) calls a "culture of memory": seeing oneself as part of a narrative thread that leads unbrokenly from "then" to "now." This story has real effects both political and commercial. "Even when the fault line between mythic past and real past is not always that easy to draw—one of the conundrums of any politics of memory anywhere," Huyssen argues, "the real can be mythologized just as the mythic may engender strong reality effects" (Huyssen, 2003: 26). Hence, Huyssen sees in nostalgia the tool for "an increasingly successful marketing of memory by the Western culture industry" (Huyssen, 2003: 25). As the glove manufacturers' product descriptions I cite earlier in this chapter attest, the "marketing of memory," is a fundamental branding strategy for the sale of baseball gloves, and many glove manufacturers make this effort to link past, present and future explicit. Indeed, many of the themes we have engaged in this chapter coalesce in Nokona's description of itself, craftsmanship, tradition, country:

> Today, Nokona is focused on the future, applying many of the same principles that have guided our past—quality, craftsmanship, innovation, integrity, and a commitment to our employees, suppliers, customers, and our country. We continue to put classic American workmanship into every glove, using techniques developed over the past 80+ years.

> (Nokona Company, 2018)

It should be lost on no one who has read this far, that much of the nostalgia engendered by a baseball glove is predominately white and male, and much of the cultural memory being marketed is about a mythic American past (even when the gloves are being manufactured overseas). If I am to be self-reflective, I often find myself seduced by that nostalgia, the idea that putting on a glove allows me to hold in my hand, some link to a heroic, virtuous, national past: Walt Whitman! Mark Twain! Gerald Early claimed that "There are only three things that America will be remembered for 2000 years from now when they study this civilization: The Constitution, Jazz music, and Baseball. These are the 3 most beautiful things this culture's ever created" (Burns et al., 1999). I can't play a musical instrument, and I'll never hold The Constitution in my hand, but I can put on a baseball glove, and feel, somehow, connected to one of the things that truly makes America great.

It's a comforting thought—especially in times like these—when the ideals embodied in The Constitution seem to be eroding.

But again—I shouldn't be seduced. The Constitution never really stood for everyone. Jazz may make America great, but Billie Holiday didn't sing "Strange Fruit" to celebrate the equality all citizens experienced. And baseball, whose racist past is well documented, didn't suddenly become a bastion of tolerance and racial justice when Jackie Robinson joined the Dodgers in 1947. Just this past season in 2017, fans of my own beloved Boston Red Sox taunted Baltimore's Manny Machado with racist slurs—70 years after the integration of MLB!

And we shouldn't forget women—forever marginalized in the annals of baseball. Forced to play a different game, with a different glove, and for the most part left out of the story I have tried to tell. Even the origin story of the glove relegates women to second-class citizens, with "sissy" players like Charlie Waite and Foxy Irving conceding something of their manhood by donning the leather. But this is the way of the nostalgia of the ball glove. Huyssen says "the real can be mythologized just as the mythic may engender strong reality effects" But *The Man who Shot Liberty Valance* put it better: "When the legend becomes fact, print the legend." Such is the allure of nostalgia.

No, if the tendency in this book has been to be seduced by the lore of the glove, the endless parades of articles with puns for titles ("Glove Affair," "Glove Story," etc.), and the continual evocation of American tradition, it is worthwhile, as we come to an end, to remember the glove stories that don't fit this narrative in hopes of telling a new one.

To be sure, there are plenty of nostalgic remembrances of baseball gloves by marginalized groups, women, people of color, and players from other countries. The former Nicaraguan Vice President, Sergio Ramírez has a lovely memoir called "Centerfield," in which he remembers his glove—which was not a baseball glove at all:

> My plaza was almost the same, with the guarumo trees next to the courtyard of the church, and me with my glove patrolling the centerfield, the only fielder who had a canvas glove was me and the rest had to catch with bare hands, and at six in the evening I continued fielding although you could hardly see but I didn't let any hit go by, and just by the sound I sensed that the ball was coming like a dove to fall in my hands.
>
> (Ramírez and Imberman, 1980: 144)

And for long-time *New York Review of Books* contributor Katherine A. Powers, her glove functioned as a means of asserting her autonomy against the patriarchal ideas of her youth:

> My oldest personal possession is my baseball glove, which I bought for eight dollars at Woolworth's in St. Cloud, Minnesota, in 1960, when I was almost 13. . . I bought this wonderful thing secretly, because my father had met the few remarks I'd made about "thinking about getting a glove" with his rote response: "You don't want that." (Other things I "didn't want"

were blue jeans, a bicycle, a penknife, a fishing pole, a permanent wave, and a pet of any sort.) A baseball glove? What would I do with it? Who would I play with? Boys at School? I was a girl.

(Powers, 2008: 163–164)

And gloves can be a totem against something else—the passage of time and the ravages of age. Throughout the book, I have referenced the fact I play baseball with an adult baseball team in Vermont. Many of the observations I have recorded about baseball gloves throughout the book have come from these men. The players range from 35 years old to over-70. With such a wide age spread, the physical capacities of the players are variable, to say the least. We jokingly call what we do "Old Man Baseball," but for some of us, the ravages of age are very real. Beyond the usual pulled muscles and torn hamstrings of the weekend warrior, it is lost on none of us that any game could be our last. A few summers ago, a player for an opposing team suffered a massive heart attack on our field immediately after a game (he survived—and still plays). This summer, one of my teammates was diagnosed with cancer, and I don't know if he'll step on the field again. For some of us, putting on a glove is like Krapp putting one more spool on his tape-recorder at the end of the Beckett play—an act of defiance against the end: "Perhaps my best years are gone. When there was a chance of happiness. But I wouldn't want them back. Not with the fire in me now. No, I wouldn't want them back." I like that better as a motto for our league than the misogyny-tinged one the National MSBL currently uses: "Don't go soft; play hardball!" Krapp might be a little wordier, but he seems more in keeping with sentiments of older players for whom putting on a glove is tantamount to resisting the passage of time and the enforced irrelevance of ageism.

There is one more thing I'd like to say about baseball gloves. Most people probably believe that you just slip the glove onto your hand. Actually, it's the other way around—you insert your hand into the glove. I know this because of my Parkinson's Disease. Sometimes I have difficulty inserting my hand into the glove; it takes the coordination of many little hand and finger muscles working together to get the glove on.

(VTMSBL player)

In the spirit of trying to tell a different story about gloves than the one this book generally has been telling, I'd like to conclude by talking about the meaning of two gloves (see Figure 3.6).

Figure 3.6 **My daughter's gloves (2017).** (*Source*: Photograph by David Jenemann.)

My daughter, Anna, has two gloves. One is a Louisville Slugger Evolution model, 11.5-inches. I bought it for her for Christmas one year while she was still in Little League. It is one of the last gloves Louisville Slugger made in America. The other is a Dong Hyuk model that Anna received in Cuba for being the fastest girl to round the bases during a baseball skills competition. To be perfectly honest, she was the only girl in the race, but she did beat a number of the boys—and she is fast. Before traveling to Cuba, I had never seen a Dong Hyuk glove before, and it is very difficult to find information about the brand. Even on the collectors' forums there is little to be learned except that some of the company's gloves mimic Rawlings—down to the slogan and lettering, and there is some conjecture that they could be knock-offs or that Dong Hyuk could be an offshore partner for Rawlings. In any case, if there is a US partner for Dong Hyuk, the fact that the only place I've ever seen a Dong Hyuk glove is in Cuba suggests that the brand is getting around the embargo by using that name only in certain markets.

We traveled to Cuba in early 2016. Anna was 12 years old and about to enter her final season of Little League. Just days after we left Havana, the first US cruise ships pulled into the harbor, signaling what many felt would be a new era of openness and a thawing of the decades-long stalemate between the US and Cuban governments.

Flash forward two years. When Anna turned twelve, she aged out of Little League, effectively ending her baseball career. She is ambivalent about softball.

The fact that she looks down on it speaks equivocally both to her feminism and to being swayed by the rhetoric about softball being a derivative "girl's game." In any case, the Louisville Slugger is now too small for her if she chooses to play softball, and softball doesn't start for her until high school. The glove hasn't caught a ball in two years.

In June 2017, President Trump announced that he was rolling back many of the Obama-era policies loosening trade and tightening relations between the US and Cuba. The embargo would—and does as of this writing—remain, a fact that merits the disapproval of nearly all of the rest of the world. It seems likely that, to the extent a player is using a new glove in Havana today, it is still a Dong Hyuk.

I look at these two gloves, and I think of the stories they tell—of how girls are marginalized in American sporting life and denied the opportunities of their male peers—of how political ideology can close down a whole country. 40 years after Title IX, girls still play on a different field, and that difference will be mirrored throughout Anna's life as she moves through her educational opportunities and into her professional career. She will often find herself playing on a different field. 60 years after the Cuban Revolution, the US is still trying to exert its dominance on our neighbor 90 miles off the coast. These gloves betoken realities much more complex than the nostalgic views of Abner Doubleday and Alexander Cartwright playing a gentleman's game in bucolic settings in the 1800s. Anna's gloves reflect a world in which there is still conflict, disagreement, poverty, misogyny and violence, and those gloves exist at a certain time, and a certain place, as do those struggles.

But these gloves also point to a world in which American girls can play baseball with Cuban boys and where the conflicts that have until now have given these gloves meaning have disappeared.

I hope to play catch with those gloves soon.

BIBLIOGRAPHY

"2016 Texas Presidential Election Results." *Politico*, December 13, 2016. www.politico.com/ 2016-election/results/map/president/texas/.

Akadema. "Babe Ruth Glove." *Product Description*. https://akademapro.com/collections/ collectables/products/babe-ruth-glove.

Akcigit, Ufuk, John Grigsby, and Tom Nicholas. "The Rise of American Ingenuity: Innovation and Inventors of the Golden Age." Working Paper Series. National Bureau of Economic Research, January 2017. www.nber.org/papers/w23047.

Alaya, Domingo. *Domingo Beisbol*. www.domingobeisbol.com/.

American Anthropological Association (AAA). "Principles of Professional Responsibility," 2012. http://ethics.americananthro.org/category/statement/.

Anderson, B. *Imagined Communities: Reflections on the Origin and Spread Of Nationalism*, 2nd Edition. London and New York: Verso, 1991.

Appadurai, Arjun, ed. *The Social Life of Things: Commodities in Cultural Perspective*. Cambridge: Cambridge University Press, 1986.

Armstrong, Gary. *Football Hooligans: Knowing the Score*. Explorations in Anthropology. Oxford and New York: Berg Books, 1998.

"A Storied History." *Spalding: About Us. Spalding Sporting Goods Company*. n.d. www.spalding. com/about-spalding.html.

Balsamo, Anne. *Designing Culture: The Technological Imagination at Work*. Durham: Duke University Press, 2011.

Barthes, Roland. *Mythologies*. Translated by Annette Lavers. The Complete Edition. New York: Hill and Wang, 1984.

Barthes, R. and Stephen Heath. *Image, Music, Text*, essays selected and translated by Stephen Heath. New York: Hill and Wang, 1977.

"Baseball-Mitt Crackdown Really a Basket Case; Gloves Off Over Size." *Edmonton Journal*, May 2, 1990. www.search.proquest.com/docview/251701255?accountid=14679.

Baudrillard, Jean. *The System of Objects*. Translated by James Benedict. New York: Verso, 1996.

Berger, Arthur Asa. *What Objects Mean: An Introduction to Material Culture*. Walnut Creek, CA: Left Coast Press, 2009.

Berlow, Lawrence H. "Baseball Glove." *How Products Are Made*, 2007. www.madehow.com/ Volume-1/Baseball-Glove.html.

Berry, John W. "Family Acculturation and Change: Recent Comparative Research." In *On New Shores: Understanding Immigrant Fathers in North America*. Edited by Susan S. Chuang and Robert P. Moreno, 25–45. Lanham, MD: Lexington Books, 2008.

Besnier, Niko, Susan Brownell, and Thomas F. Carter. *The Anthropology of Sport: Bodies, Borders, Biopolitics*. Berkeley and London: University of California Press, 2017.

Blanchard, Kendall. *The Anthropology of Sport: An Introduction*. 2nd Edition. Santa Barbara: Bergin and Garvey, 1995.

Boradkar, Prasad. *Designing Things: A Critical Introduction to the Culture of Objects*. New York: Berg Publishers, 2010.

Bourdieu, Pierre. *Distinction: A Social Critique of the Judgement of Taste.* Cambridge: Harvard University Press, 1984.

Bourdieu, Pierre. *In Other Words: Essays Towards a Reflexive Sociology.* Stanford: Stanford University Press, 1990.

Bourdieu, Pierre. "How Can One Be a Sports Fan?" In *The Cultural Studies Reader.* Edited by Simon During, 427–440. London and New York: Routledge, 1999.

Bradlee Jr., Ben. *The Kid: The Immortal Life of Ted Williams.* Boston: Little, Brown, and Co., 2013.

"Breaking in a Glove with Aso." *YouTube Video,* 7:27. Posted by BaseballMonkey. October 22, 2015. www.youtube.com/watch?v=cGFcHjRSad4.

Brock, Darryl. "Mark Twain, Baseball Fan, Had an Eye for a Short-Stop." *The New York Times,* March 13, 2010. www.nytimes.com/2010/03/14/sports/baseball/14twain.html?mcubz=0.

Brown, Bill. "Waging Baseball, Playing War: Games of American Imperialism." *Cultural Critique* no. 17 (1990–91): 51–78. doi: 10.2307/1354139.

Brown, Brandon and Gregg Bennett "Baseball is Whack: Exploring the Lack of African American Baseball Consumption." *Journal of Sport and Social Issues* 39, no. 4 (2015): 287–307. doi: 10.1177/0193723514561550.

Brown, Harry. *Golf Ball. Object Lessons.* New York: Bloomsbury, 2015.

Bruner, Jerome. "The Narrative Construction of Reality." *Critical Inquiry* 18, no. 1 (1991): 1–21. www.jstor.org/stable/1343711.

Buckley, Christopher. "Nostalgia: The 1950s and My Mitts." In *Anatomy of Baseball.* Edited by Lee Gutkind and Andrew Blauner, 85–98. Dallas: Southern Methodist University Press, 2008.

Burns, K., Florentine Films, PBS Video and WETA-TV. Baseball (video recording), a production of Florentine Films; WETA; a film by Ken Burns; produced by Ken Burns and Lynn Novick; written by Geoffrey C. Ward and Ken Burns (PBS Video index version. ed., PBS Video database of America's history & culture; v. 107–124). Alexandria, VA: PBS Video, 1999.

Butler, Judith. "Performative Acts and Gender Constitution: An Essay in Phenomenology and Feminist Theory." *Theater Journal* 40, no. 4 (1988): 519–531. doi: 10.2307/3207893.

Campbell, Peter A. *Old-Time Base Ball and the First Modern World Series.* Brookfield, CT: The Millbrook Press, Inc., 2002.

Certeau, Michel de. *The Practice of Everyday Life.* Berkeley: University of California Press, 1984.

Chin, Ken. "Hermes is Selling a Hand Stitched Baseball Glove for $14,100." *Bleacher Report,* April 11, 2014. www.bleacherreport.com/articles/2026114-hermes-is-selling-a-hand-stitched-baseball-glove-for-14100.

Chrzan, Janet. *Alcohol: Social Drinking in Cultural Context.* Routledge Series for Creative Teaching and Learning in Anthropology. New York: Routledge, 2013.

Coleman, Gabriella E. "Hacker Practice: Moral Genres and the Cultural Articulation of Liberalism." *Anthropological Theory* 8, no. 3 (2008): 255–277.

Coleman, Gabriella E. "The Anthropology of Hackers." *The Atlantic,* September 21, 2010. www.theatlantic.com/technology/archive/2010/09/the-anthropology-of-hackers/63308/.

Cooper, Joseph, Joey Gawrusiak, and Billy Hawkins. "Racial Perceptions of Baseball at Historically Black Colleges and Universities." *Journal of Sport and Social Issues* 37, no. 2 (2012): 196–221. doi: 10.1177/0193723512455921.

Daniel, Dan. "A.L. Balks Over Rule on Bringing Gloves Off Field." *The Sporting News,* March 24, 1954.

de Lauretis, Teresa. *Alice Doesn't: Feminism, Semiotics, Cinema.* Bloomington, IN: Indiana University Press, 1984.

de Saussure, Ferdinand. *Course in General Linguistics.* Translated by Wade Baskin. Edited by Charles Bally, Albert Sechehaye, and Albert Riedlinger. New York: McGraw-Hill, 1966.

Doak, William L. U.S. Patent 1,426,824A filed April 18, 1921, and issued August 22, 1922.

Dubisch, Jill. "Run for the Wall: An American Pilgrimage." In *Conformity and Conflict: Readings in Cultural Anthropology*. Edited by James P. Spradley and David W. McCurdy, 14th Edition, 275–286. London: Pearson, 2012.

Eastman, Benjamin, Sean Brown, and Michael Ralph, eds. *America's Game(s): A Critical Anthropology of Sport*. New York: Routledge, 2013.

Eiss, Paul and David E. Pedersen. "Introduction: Values of Value." *Cultural Anthropology* 17, no. 3 (2002): 283–290.

Elias, Robert. *The Empire Strikes Out: How Baseball Sold U.S. Foreign Policy and Promoted the American Way Abroad*. New York: The New Press, 2010.

Ellard, Harry. *Baseball in Cincinnati: A History*. Cincinnati: Press of Johnson & Hardin, 1907.

Fadiman, A. *The Spirit Catches You and You Fall Down: A Hmong Child, Her American Doctors, and the Collison of Two Cultures*. New York: Farrar, Straus & Giroux, 2012.

Fatsis, Stefan. "My Glove: A Biography." In *Anatomy of Baseball*. Edited by Lee Gutkind and Andrew Blauner, 15–34. Dallas: Southern Methodist University Press, 2008.

Ferguson, Eugene S. "On the Origin and Development of American Mechanical 'Know-How'." *American Studies* 3, no. 2 (1962): 3–16.

Foucault, Michel. *Archaeology of Knowledge*. Translated by A.M. Sheridan Smith. New York: Routledge, 2002.

Freeman, Rodney, Katherine C. Donahue, Eric Baxter, Patrick J. Collins, Marie Connell, and Steven Kantor. "The Draper–Maynard Sporting Goods Company of Plymouth, New Hampshire, 1840–1937." *IA. The Journal of the Society for Industrial Archeology* 20, no. ½ (1994): 139–151. www.jstor.org/stable/40968288.

Gearty, Robert and Larry McShane. "Fraudster Yankee Memorabilia Peddler Busted for Selling Fake Babe Ruth Glove on eBay Gets Easy Sentence." *New York Daily News*, December 23, 2012 www.nydailynews.com/sports/baseball/yankees/memorabilia-imposter-busted-selling-fake-babe-ruth-glove-article-1.1224841.

Gmelch, George. "Baseball Magic." *Transaction* 8 (1971): 39–41, 54.

Gmelch, George. "The Rituals of Baseball." *The Washington Post*, July 16, 1978. www.washington post.com/archive/opinions/1978/07/16/the-rituals-of-baseball/520382d5-2b17-4480-8574-442f380a6c00/?utm_term=.2543cc662592.

Gmelch, George. "Superstition and Ritual in American Baseball." *Elysian Fields Quarterly* 11, no. 3 (1992): 25–36.

Gmelch, George. *Inside Pitch: Life in Professional Baseball*. Washington, DC: Smithsonian Institution Press, 2001.

Gmelch, George. "An Anthropologist on the Team: Studying Baseball as a Former Player." *Anthropology Today*, 24 (2008): 10–15.

Graves-Brown, Paul, ed. *Matter, Materiality and Modern Culture*. London: Routledge, 2000.

Gunn, Wendy, Ton Otto, and Rachel Charlotte Smith, eds. *Design Anthropology: Theory and Practice*. London and New York: Bloomsbury Academic, 2013.

Gutman, Dan and Tim McCarver. *The Way Baseball Works*. New York: Simon & Schuster, 1996.

Gwynne, S.C. "Glove Story." *Texas Monthly*, March, 2007. www.texasmonthly.com/articles/glove-story/.

Harbach, Chad. *The Art of Fielding: A Novel*. New York: Little, Brown, and Co., 2011.

Hartley, Leslie Poles. *The Go-Between*. New York: New York Review Books, 2002.

Hebdige, Dick. *Subculture, the Meaning of Style*. New Accents. London: Methuen, 1979.

Hegel, Georg, and Johannes Hoffmeister. Lectures on the philosophy of world history: Introduction: Reason in history / Georg Wilhelm Friedrich Hegel; translated from the German edition of Johannes Hoffmeister by H. B. Nisbet, with an introduction by Duncan Forbes (Cambridge studies in the history and theory of politics). Cambridge and New York: Cambridge University Press, 1975.

Heidegger, Martin. *Being and Time*. Translated by John Macquarrie and Edward Robinson. New York: Harper, 1962.

Heidegger, Martin. *Poetry, Language, Thought*. Translation and introduction by Albert Hofstadter. New York: Harper & Row, 1975.

Horner, Jack. "Rookie Devises Huge Glove to 'Hide Pitches and Protect His Legs'—Praying it is Legal." *Greensboro (NC) Daily News*, April 13, 1939.

"How It's Made Baseball Gloves." *YouTube Video*, 5:02. Posted by How It's Made. April 19, 2015. www.youtube.com/watch?v=PtySoTctqmk.

"How to Custom Baseball Gloves | Angelus Paint." *YouTube Video*, 7:20. Posted by Angelus Shoe Polish. May 19, 2016. www.youtube.com/watch?v=KD7JoTtr59s.

"How to Customize Your Baseball Glove—Pimp My Glove." *YouTube Video*, 3:44. Posted by YouGoPro. March 26, 2010. www.youtube.com/watch?v=44MZPwESxvg.

"How to Make a Custom Baseball Glove with a Heat Press and Vinyl Cutter TRW." *YouTube Video*, 7:19. TheRhinestoneWorld. February 17, 2015. www.youtube.com/watch?v=WK-MWED0tAss.

Hume, D., Thomas Hodge Grose and Thomas Hill Green. *A Treatise on Human Nature: Being an Attempt to Introduce the Experimental Method of Reasoning into Moral Subjects and Dialogues Concerning Natural Religion*. London: Longmans, Green, 1878.

Hutcheon, Linda. "Irony, Nostalgia, and the Postmodern." *University of Toronto English Language (UTEL) Main Collection*, 1998 www.library.utoronto.ca/utel/criticism/hutchinp.html.

Huyssen, Andreas. *Present Pasts: Urban Palimpsests and the Politics of Memory*. Stanford: Stanford University Press, 2003.

Ingold, Tim. "Making Culture and Weaving the World." In *Matter, Materiality and Modern Culture*. Edited by P. Graves-Brown, 50–71. London: Routledge, 2000.

Ingold, Tim. "The Textility of Making." *Cambridge Journal of Economics* 34 (2010): 91–102.

Ingold, Tim. *Making: Anthropology, Archaeology, Art and Architecture*. London: Taylor & Francis, 2013.

Irwin, Arthur Albert. *Player File*. Compiled by the National Baseball Hall of Fame Library, n.d. Cooperstown, New York.

Irwin, Arthur A. *Practical Ball Playing*. New York: American Sports Publishing Company, 1895.

Jameson, Frederic. *Postmodernism, or, The Cultural Logic of Late Capitalism*. Durham: Duke University Press, 1991.

Johnson, Chuck. "Enforcement Web to Extend to Oversized Fielders' Mitts." *USA TODAY*, March 27, 1990. www.search.proquest.com/docview/306306362?accountid=14679.

Johnson, Chuck. "Glove Size Rule to be Hands-on." *USA TODAY*, 1990. www.search.proquest.com/docview/306303238?accountid=14679.

Kaham, Oscar. "Rule Rewritten to Clamp Curb on the Use of Oversize Gloves." *Sporting News*, May 6, 1972.

Kahneman, Daniel. *Thinking, Fast and Slow*. New York: Farrar, Straus, and Giroux, 2011.

Keane, Webb. "Semiotics and the Social Analysis of Material Things." *Language & Communication* 23 (2003): 409–425.

Klein, Alan M. *Sugarball: The American Game, The Dominican Dream*. New Haven, CT: Yale University Press, 1991.

Kopytoff, Igor. "The Cultural Biography of Things: Commoditization as Process." In *The Social Life of Things*. Edited by Arjun Appadurai, 64–94. Cambridge: Cambridge University Press, 1986.

Kurkjian, Tim. "Old-Fashioned Glove Story." *ESPN The Magazine*, March 21, 2002. www.espn.com/magazine/kurkjian_20020321.html.

Kusaka, Yuko. "The Development of Baseball Organizations in Japan." *International Review for Sociology of Sport* 22, no. 4 (1987): 263–278.

Lamster, Mark. *Spalding's World Tour: The Epic Adventure that Took Baseball Around the Globe—And Made it America's Game*. New York: Public Affairs Press, 2006.

Lang, Jack. "Orioles Build Better Mousetrap—Catch Butterflies." *Long Island Press*, May 28, 1960.

Lasch, Christopher. *The True and Only Heaven: Progress and Its Critics*. New York: W.W. Norton Press, 1991.

Latour, Bruno. "The Berlin Key or How to Do Words with Things." In *Matter, Materiality and Modern Culture*. Edited by P. Graves-Brown, 10–22. London: Routledge, 2000.

Lee, Jason. "Akadema: Innovation on the Diamond." In *Branded: Branding in Sport Business.* Edited by Jason Lee, 13–22. Durham: Carolina Academic Press, 2010.

Lefton, Brad. "Ichiro's Gloves–The Hands of a Master." *Seattle Times,* July 25, 2008. www.seattletimes. com/sports/mariners/ichiros-glove-8212-the-hands-of-a-master/.

Le Goff, Jacques. *The Medieval Imagination,* translated by Arthur Goldhammer. Chicago: University of Chicago Press, 1988.

Lemonnier, Pierre. *Mundane Objects: Materiality and Non-Verbal Communication.* Walnut Creek, CA: Left Coast Press, 2012.

Lenza, Michael. "Controversies Surrounding Laud Humphreys' Tearoom Trade: An Unsettling Example of Politics and Power in Methodological Critiques." *International Journal of Sociology and Social Policy* 24, no. 3/4/5 (2004): 20–31.

Lewis, Michael. *Moneyball: The Art of Winning an Unfair Game.* New York: W.W. Norton Press, 2004.

Liberman, Noah. *Glove Affairs: The Romance, History, and Tradition of the Baseball Glove.* Chicago: Triumph Books, 2003.

Light, Jonathan Fraser. *The Cultural Encyclopedia of Baseball.* 2nd Edition. Jefferson, NC: McFarland Incorporated Publishers, 2005.

Lindholm, Karl. "A-ha! Moments' and the Cuban Giants." *Addison Independent,* August 11, 2016. www.addisonindependent.com/201608karl-linholm-ha-moments-and-cuban-giants.

LinWeber, Ralph E. "Baseball Guides Galore." *Society for American Baseball Research.* Cronkite School at ASU, n.d. www.research.sabr.org/journals/baseball-guides-galore.

Marx, Karl and Friedrich Engels. *Capital: A Critique of Political Economy.* Translated by Edward Aveling and Samuel Moore. Chicago: Charles H. Kerr & Company, 1915.

Matteson, Jesse F. *How to Play the Outfield.* New York: American Sports Publishing Company, 1905.

Mauss, Marcel. "Techniques of the body." *Economy and Society* 2 (1973): 70–88.

Mayeda, Andrew. "The Last American Baseball-Glove Maker Refuses to Die." *Bloomberg,* August 14, 2017. www.bloomberg.com/news/features/2017-08-14/the-last-american-baseball-glove-maker-refuses-to-die.

McGunnigle, Bill. *Pioneer Baseball.* Scrapbook. National Baseball Hall of Fame and Museum, 1878.

Mertz, Elizabeth. "Semiotic Anthropology." *Annual Review of Anthropology* 36, no. 1 (2007): 337–353.

Miller, Daniel. *Material Culture and Mass Consumption.* Oxford, UK and New York: B. Blackwell, 1987.

Miller, Daniel. *Material Cultures: Why Some Things Matter.* New York: Taylor & Francis, 2002.

Miller, Daniel. *Materiality,* edited by Daniel Miller. Durham: Duke University Press, 2005.

Miller, Daniel. *Stuff.* Cambridge: Polity Press, 2010.

Miller, Michael. "American Football: The Rationalization of the Irrational." *International Journal of Politics, Culture, and Society* 11, no. 1 (1997): 101–127.

Moore, David Leon. "Japanese: An Instant Glove." *Rochester Democrat and Chronicle,* July 1, 1981.

Morgan, Joe. *Baseball for Dummies,* 4th Edition. Indianapolis: John Wiley and Sons, 2014.

Morris, Peter. *A Game of Inches: The Stories Behind the Innovations that Shaped Baseball.* Chicago: Ivan R. Dee, Publisher, 2010.

Morris, Peter. "Ben De La Vergne." Society for American Baseball Research. Cronkite School at ASU, n.d. www.sabr.org/bioproj/person/3232b51c#_edn1.

Murdock, George Peter. "Waging Baseball on Truk." In *Culture and Society: Twenty-Four Essays,* George Peter Murdock, 290–293. Pittsburgh: University of Pittsburgh Press, 1965.

National Baseball Hall of Fame and Brooks Robinson. *Inside the Baseball Hall of Fame.* New York: Simon & Schuster, 2013.

National Baseball Hall of Fame and Museum. Clippings File "Baseball Gloves."

National Baseball Hall of Fame and Museum. *"Owe'd 2 Base Ball in Three Cant-oh's!"* Philadelphia: McLaughlin Brothers, 1860.

National Security Archive. "Beisbol Diplomacy." *National Security Archive Electronic Briefing Book No. 12*, n.d. https://nsarchive2.gwu.edu//NSAEBB/NSAEBB12/nsaebb12.htm.

Nightengale, Bob. "Number of African-American Baseball Players Dips Again." *USA TODAY*, April 16, 2012. www.usatoday30.usatoday.com/sports/baseball/story/2012-04-15/baseball-jackie-robinson/54302108/1.

Nokona Company. "Our Story." www.nokona.com/about, 2018.

"Nokona." *Vendor Description*. Just Ball Gloves, n.d. www.justballgloves.com/vendors/nokona/.

O'Connor, Kaori *Lycra: How a Fiber Shaped America* (Routledge series for creative teaching and learning in anthropology). New York: Routledge, 2011.

Office of the Commissioner of Baseball. "Official Baseball Rules 2017 Edition," 2017. http://mlb.mlb.com/documents/0/4/0/224919040/2017_Official_Baseball_Rules_dbt69t59.pdf.

Ogden, David C. "The Welcome Theory: An Approach to Studying African American Youth Interest and Involvement in Baseball." *Nine: A Journal of Baseball History & Culture* 12, no. 2 (2004): 114–122.

O'Keefe, Michael. "BUYER BEWARE Crystal's Glove Affair a Lesson for Mantle Auction." *New York Daily News*, December 7, 2003. www.nydailynews.com/archives/sports/buyer-beware-crystal-glove-affair-lesson-mantle-auction-article-1.514248.

Okely, Judith. *Anthropological Practice: Fieldwork and the Ethnographic Method*. Oxford: Berg Publishers, 2011.

Otto, Ton and Rachel Charlotte Smith. "Design Anthropology: A Distinct Style of Knowing." In *Design Anthropology: Theory and Practice*. Edited by Wendy Gunn, Ton Otto, and Rachel Charlotte Smith, 1–27. New York: Bloomsbury Academic, 2013.

Paine, Neil and Carl Bialik. "The Gold Gloves Are Finally Going to the Best Fielders." *FiveThirtyEight*, November 11, 2015. www.fivethirtyeight.com/features/the-gold-gloves-are-finally-going-to-the-best-fielders/.

Peters, Henry J. "Changes in Official Playing Rules." Correspondence. *National Baseball Hall of Fame*, April 3, 1972.

Poliquin, Bud. "Poliquin: A Reader/Writer Wonders When Baseball Players Stopped Leaving Their Gloves Behind." *Syracuse*, May 13, 2013. www.syracuse.com/poliquin/index.ssf/2013/05/poliquin_a_readerwriter_wonder_1.html.

Povich, Shirley. "Many Cuss New Rule in Bringing in Gloves." *The Sporting News*, March 17, 1954.

Powers, Katherine A. "My Glove." In *Anatomy of Baseball*. Edited by Lee Gutkind and Andrew Blauner, 163–70. Dallas: Southern Methodist University Press, 2008.

Preston, Beth. "The Function of Things: A Philosophical Perspective on Material Culture." In *Matter, Materiality and Modern Culture*. Edited by P. Graves-Brown, 72–96. London: Routledge, 2000.

"Principles of Professional Responsibility." *American Anthropology Association Ethics Blog (blog)*. November 1, 2012. www.ethics.americananthro.org/category/statement/.

Ramírez, Sergio and Flaurie S. Imberman. "The Centerfielder." *Latin American Perspectives* 7, no. 2–3 (1980): 140–144.

Rawlings, George H. Glove. U.S. Patent 325,968A filed March 1885, and issued September 8, 1885.

Rawlings Sporting Goods. "Gold Glove 12 in. Infield, Pitcher Glove." *Product Description*, n.d. www.rawlings.com/product/P-RGG206-4B.html.

Richtel, Matt. *A Deadly Wandering: A Mystery, A Landmark Investigation, and the Astonishing Science of Attention in the Digital Age*. New York: William Morrow, 2015.

Rivoli, Pietra. *The Travels of a T-Shirt in the Global Economy: An Economist Examines the Markets, Power, and Politics of World Trade*. 2nd Edition. Hoboken, NJ: John Wiley, 2009.

Robinson, Phil A. (Director). *Field of Dreams* (video file), 1989.

Roosevelt, Theodore. "The Manly Virtues and Practical Politics." In *The Forum*. Edited by Lorettus Sutton Metcalf, Walter Hines Page, Joseph Mayer Rice, Frederic Taber Cooper,

Arthur Hooley, Mitchell Kennerley, Edwin Wildman, George Henry Payne, and Henry Goddard Leach, 549–557. New York: Forum Publishing Company, 1886.

Rushin, Steve. *The 34-Ton Bat: The Story of Baseball as Told Through Bobbleheads, Cracker Jacks, Jockstraps, Eye Black, and 375 Other Strange and Unforgettable Objects.* Boston: Little, Brown, and Co., 2013.

Ryczek, William. "The Origins of the Art of Pitching During the 19th Century." *The National Pastime Museum,* December 1, 2012. www.thenationalpastimemuseum.com/article/origins-art-pitching-during-19th-century-0.

Salinger, J.D. *The Catcher in the Rye.* Boston: Little, Brown, and Co., 2001.

Schiffer, Michael Brian. "Indigenous Theories, Scientific Theories and Product Histories. In *Matter, Materiality and Modern Culture.* Edited by P. Graves-Brown, 72–96. London: Routledge, 2000.

Schultz, Jeff. "Glove Warfare: Umpires Crack Down on Illegal Equipment." *The Ottawa Citizen,* May 2, 1990. www.search.proquest.com/docview/239467954?accountid=14679.

Schwarz, Alan. "Left-Handed and Left Out." *The New York Times,* August 15, 2009. www.nytimes.com/2009/08/16/sports/baseball/16catcher.html.

Seideman, David. "A Rare and Valuable Vintage Lou Gehrig Baseball Mitt Is a Holy Grail." *Forbes,* July 14, 2014. www.forbes.com/sites/davidseideman/2014/07/14/a-rare-and-valuable-lou-gehrig-baseball-mitt-is-a-holy-grail/#504d263a6407.

Seideman, David. "Talk About Hidden Treasure: $11.6K Babe Ruth Baseball Glove Found in Old Chest in Norway." *Forbes,* March 28, 2017. www.forbes.com/sites/davidseideman/2017/03/28/talk-about-hidden-treasure-valuable-baseball-memorabilia-found-in-old-chest-in-norway/#6eb3b6681324.

Selcraig, Bruce. "Glove Story/Few Things are Sacred in a Major League Clubhouse, but (Just ask Barry Bonds) You Don't Mess with a Man's Mitt." *FORBES,* March 5, 2001, 84–89.

Sennett, Richard. *The Craftsmen.* New Haven, CT: Yale University Press, 2008.

Sharkey-Gotlieb, Simon. "Rizzo Becomes 1st Left-Handed Throwing Third Baseman Since 1997." *The Score,* August 22, 2017. www.thescore.com/news/1356687.

Shore, Bradd. "Marginal Play: Sport at the Borderlands of Time and Space." *International Review for Sociology of Sport* 29, no. 4 (1994): 349–365.

Simon, Tom, ed. *Deadball Stars of the National League.* Washington, DC: Brassey's, Inc., 2004.

Spalding, Albert G. *America's National Game.* New York: American Sports Publishing Company, 1911.

Spalding Guide, *Spalding's Official Base Ball Guide,* 1895. www.loc.gov/item/spalding.00148/.

Spradley, James. *The Ethnographic Interview.* New York: Holt, Rinehart, and Winston, 1979.

Stallybrass, Peter and Ann Rosalind Jones. "Fetishizing the Glove in Renaissance Europe." *Critical Inquiry* 28, no. 1 (2001): 114–132.

Stamp, Jimmy. "The Invention of the Baseball Mitt." *Smithsonian Magazine,* July 16, 2013. www.smithsonianmag.com/arts-culture/the-invention-of-the-baseball-mitt-12799848/.

Steinberg, Steve. "Bill Doak." *Society for American Baseball Research.* Cronkite School at ASU, 2004. www.sabr.org/bioproj/person/1359e4e2.

Stewart, Kathleen. "Nostalgia—A Polemic." *Cultural Anthropology* 3, no. 3 (1988): 227–241.

Stewart, Susan. *On Longing: Narratives of the Miniature, the Gigantic, the Souvenir, the Collection.* Durham: Duke University Press, 1993.

Summers, Eleanor M. *Raising a Reader: Improving Reading and Writing Skills (Grade 4).* Napanee, Ontario: Simon & Schuster Learning Materials, 2011.

Thorn, John. *Baseball in the Garden of Eden: The Secret History of the Early Game.* New York: Simon & Schuster, 2011.

Traubel, Horace. *With Walt Whitman in Camden, Volume 1.* Edited by Sculley Bradley, Boston: Small, Maynard, and Company, 1906.

Tucker, Catherine. *Coffee Culture: Local Experiences, Global Connections.* Routledge Series for Creative Teaching and Learning in Anthropology. New York: Routledge, 2011.

"Umpires Get Tough on Glove Size Today." *USA TODAY,* 1990. www.search.proquest.com/docview/306338105?accountid=14679.

Vivanco, Luis A. *Reconsidering the Bicycle: An Anthropological Perspective on a New (Old) Thing.* New York: Routledge, 2013.

Wark, McKenzie. "A Hacker Manifesto [Version 4.0]." *Subsol* (blog), 2017. www.subsol.c3.hu/subsol_2/contributors0/warktext.html.

Weiser, Benjamin. "Man Faces Prison for Selling Glove with Babe Ruth Lie." *The New York Times,* June 28, 2012. www.nytimes.com/2012/06/29/nyregion/man-faces-prison-for-selling-glove-with-babe-ruth-lie.html.

Welsch, Robert L. and Luis A. Vivanco. *Asking Questions About Cultural Anthropology: A Concise Introduction.* New York: Oxford University Press, 2015.

Werzer, Martin. "Japanese Mitts a Hit on U.S. Diamonds." *Observer-Dispatch,* March 25, 1979.

White, Hayden V. *Tropics of Discourse: Essays in Cultural Criticism.* Baltimore: Johns Hopkins University Press, 1978.

"Why Sears Signed Ted Williams—As a Playing Manager." *Sports Illustrated* March 5, 1962. www.si.com/vault/1962/03/05/620662/why-sears-signed-ted-williamsas-a-playing-manager.

Wilson Sporting Goods. "2018 A2K 1787 11.75." *Product Description,* n.d. www.wilson.com/en-us/baseball/gloves/infield/a2k-1787-glove-right-hand-throw-11-75-in.

Witz, Billy. "To Break in Their Gloves, Yankees Dunk, Tenderize and Lather Up." *The New York Times,* March 7, 2015. www.nytimes.com/2015/03/08/sports/baseball/to-break-in-their-gloves-yankees-dunk-tenderize-and-lather-up.html?_r=0.

Woodward, Ian. *Understanding Material Culture.* New York: Sage Publication Ltd., 2007.

Wulf, Steve. "Glove Story." *Sports Illustrated,* May 7, 1990. www.si.com/vault/1990/05/07/106781448/glove-story.

INDEX

Made in the USA
Monee, IL
13 June 2023

35743721R00096